HISTORICAL HEARTTHROBS

HISTORICAL HEARTTHROBS

50 TIMELESS CRUSHES—*from* CLEOPATRA *to* CAMUS

KELLY MURPHY *with* HALLIE FRYD

35 Stillman Street, Suite 121
San Francisco, CA 94107
www.zestbooks.net

Text copyright © 2013 Kelly Murphy

Young Adult Nonfiction / People & Places / General
Library of Congress control number: 2013936872
ISBN: 978-1-936976-10-2

Front cover design: Tracy Johnson
Interior and jacket design: Tanya Napier

Manufactured in China
SCP 10 9 8 7 6 5 4 3 2 1
4500433373

Connect with Zest!
zestbooks.net/blog
zestbooks.net/contests
twitter.com/zestbooks
facebook.com/zestbook
facebook.com/BooksWithATwist
pinterest.com/zestbooks

❁

For MM and DM

CONTENTS

INTRODUCTION

If you were anything like I was in school, history class probably functioned as a time to refine your deeply considered sketch of a monkey dangling from a palm tree in outer space, or perhaps for wondering whether you remembered both your mouth guard and your cleats. The stereotype of history class as a mind-numbingly dull endeavor often has more than a grain of truth to it—especially when your teacher's monotonous voice is about as captivating as the grayscale paisley on his tie. So how can we make history come to life? It's simple: Add some romance.

Way back in elementary school, we learned that history is the record and interpretation of past events, documenting important objects, places, and of course, people. Ambrose Bierce offered his own definition of history as, "An account, mostly false, of events, mostly unimportant, which are brought about by rulers, mostly knaves, and soldiers, mostly fools." It's a cynical outlook on the course of human events, but it does hint at one of the things that makes history compelling—the people! Historical figures are still people, they just wore funnier clothes and didn't have the internet. And much like people today, the nature of their hotness varied, from physical to intellectual to emotional. At first glance, rating the hotness of some of history's most influential people might seem shallow or reductive, but when you think about it, a person's level of attractiveness can really help or hinder their influence on the world around them.

While there's just no way to make a definitive list of the 50 hottest historical figures of all time—because one person's hottie is another person's nottie—I can at least explain my basic rationale behind the selection process. In general, I tried to include historical figures for whom there were some accurate (and flattering) representations available. (Because it's one thing to say "Nikola Tesla was a smoking hot scientist," but it's something else entirely to feel the power of his trademark smirk.) This meant, for the most part, that the Ancient world was off limits, but Cleopatra snuck in because the legend of her beauty was a major part of her appeal both in her time and today.

Historical Heartthrobs includes hotties from a variety of eras, countries, and spheres of influence. For instance, you'll find the usual influential suspects, like politicians and generals, but you'll also read about the scientists, activists, entertainers, and even pilots who made an impact on the world. And while we're on the subject of diversity, some of the people included here are immediately, obviously, heart-throbbingly attractive, while others might not be your cup of tea physically, but their intellect or legacy is just as attractive as another hottie's body.

If you have ever read a newspaper or watched a reality show, then you already know that hotness doesn't necessarily equal goodness. In fact, sometimes hotness is even increased by certain diabolical tendencies. As a result, *Historical Heartthrobs* includes people (like Frederick Douglass) who fought bravely and tirelessly for social progress and change, and others (like Bugsy Siegel) who would do just about anything (and kill anyone) to make a buck. The common thread? One way or another, the 50 people in this book made other people swoon. Each entry explains why these people were sexy to their contemporaries and why they still matter to us today, sometimes for better (as in the case of Jane Goodall) and sometimes for worse (as in the case of John Wilkes Booth).

To prevent broken hearts, I've provided a handy "heat index" that evaluates the pros (bravery, intelligence, wit) and cons (narcissism, rudeness, assassin-y tendencies) of each historical heartthrob. Indispensable fun facts and quotes help reveal what hanging with these heartthrobs in their respective day and age was really like. And, of course, each entry includes an incredible image of each figure doing what they do best—lookin' good and makin' history in the process.

There's not a dull person in the bunch, so if a page or two isn't enough to satisfy your curiosity about Frida Kahlo or Huey Newton, turn to the further reading section (see page 212) to help fan the flames of your new love affairs.

Historical Heartthrobs is written for history buffs and beginners alike. At its core, it's an appreciation of people who figured out what they were passionate about—be it aviation, poker, or just other people—and turned it into something powerful. At the end of the day, isn't that what we all dream of?

CLEOPATRA

VITAL STATS

YEARS: *70/69 BCE – 30 BCE*

COUNTRY OF ORIGIN: *Egypt*

AREA OF INFLUENCE: *Politics*

STYLE OF SEDUCTION:
Shakin' things up, keepin' things fresh

N<u>o</u> 1

In art, plays, and films over the centuries, the life of Cleopatra has taken on an almost mythic quality due to the volatile nature of her love life, but at the root of her fame was her political power as the last real leader of the Macedonian dynasty in Egypt.

⇨ CLEOPATRA'S LIFE STORY

Born in Alexandria, Egypt, in the first century BCE, Cleopatra was the daughter of King Ptolemy XII Auletes. In an atmosphere where royal hierarchy was of the utmost importance, her youth was spent preparing for her ascension to the throne. Upon her father's death, she accepted the queendom with her teen brother—and husband—Ptolemy XIII, but the power struggle proved too much for the siblings. When Cleopatra attempted to oust Ptolemy XIII from the throne, he took revenge by having her run out of the palace in Alexandria. (Talk about annoying little brothers!) Cleopatra wasn't having it, though, and removed all mention of Ptolemy XIII from every legal document in her home and otherwise refused to acknowledge him until the fateful day when she was exiled to Syria by "he who could not be named." At this point, Cleopatra had had enough of these internal squabbles and sought help from the most powerful force on the planet at the time: the Roman Empire. It wasn't going to be easy to gain access to the emperor, but Cleopatra had an idea that was possessed of both practicality and panache. Legend has it that she had herself delivered, inside a rug, directly to Julius Caesar himself—and finding herself in his presence, she immediately began to plead her case.

Once she had the Roman dictator's support (not to mention that of the massive army she had built up while in Syria), Cleopatra renewed her assault on the throne. By the time the fighting was over, her brother had drowned in the Nile and she was back in business—and in power. Although Egyptian law did not allow Cleopatra, as a woman, to rule alone, she was able to skirt this legal hindrance by marrying another brother, Ptolemy XIV, which, however, did nothing to disrupt her romance with Caesar. Caesar and Cleopatra took a famous trip down the Nile together, and Cleopatra subsequently gave birth to a son (whom historians assume was Caesar's) in June, 47 BCE. When Caesar was assassinated in court, the coquettish Cleo headed back to Egypt and soon revived her spirits (and her prospects) by forming a new alliance with Caesar's presumed successor, Mark Antony. And as if she weren't already busy enough, she managed, between trysts, to keep Egypt independent and thriving—a thorny task amid a Roman Empire eager to dominate—and quickly rose in power. Her loyalty to Antony was now cemented by the births of their three children, and she put into place trading systems with India and Arabia to boost the ancient equivalent of Egypt's GDP.

In the end, however, the alliance between Mark Antony and Cleopatra wasn't strong enough to resist the powerful alliance of the Roman Senate and their own candidate for power, Octavian (later Caesar Augustus). Cleopatra's life always had a lot of drama, but in the end it became a tragedy: Antony stabbed himself to death in 30 BCE, and Cleopatra followed in his wake, allegedly committing suicide by snakebite. (Yowch!)

ELIZABETH TAYLOR PORTRAYAL

Among the dozens of on-screen portrayals of Cleopatra, the most memorable was that of Elizabeth Taylor in the 1963 film *Cleopatra*. With her hair in a black braided wig accompanied by an elaborate gold headpiece, Taylor gave a performance that cemented Cleopatra's reputation as a gorgeous seductress in the public's mind.

⇨ THE STORY OF HER SEX LIFE

Cleopatra's sex life *was* her political life, and vice versa. She used every resource at her disposal in her effort to consolidate her own personal power and to help Egypt survive a period of great upheaval.

Still, leaving aside for a moment her accomplishments, the list of names in her little black book is truly startling: Though her marriage to her brother constitutes her first romantic relationship in principle, there was little romance to be found there, judging from her legendary dalliances. After he was set aside, she moved on to Julius Caesar, the preeminent Roman dictator and perhaps the only other person whose power could match her own. From the day she literally rolled into his court, she had him wrapped around her finger, and they matched each other not only in dark wit but also, conveniently, in political agendas. After a visit to Cleopatra's native land, Caesar was floored by its efficiency and used Cleopatra's Egypt as a model for his own reforms in Rome.

With a reputation for admiring strong and capable women (which was unusual in ancient Rome), Mark Antony was the perfect match for the wayward Cleopatra once Caesar was out of the picture. They were a match made in heaven until they met their hellish end.

⇨ WHY SHE MATTERS

Cleopatra was an intelligent, pragmatic, and politically astute ruler at a time when positions of power were generally just *not held* by women.

And although her legacy has shifted over time (reflecting, by turns, the Roman view, the Egyptian view, the romantic and cinematic prejudices, and the still developing historical record), she did, very clearly, "change the face of the world"—to borrow the words of Blaise Pascal. She fought for Egyptian independence at a time when Rome appeared ready to swallow the known world, worked to make the Egyptian economy more dynamic, and managed relations between East and West like few rulers have before or since. She was irreplaceable.

⇗ BEST FEATURE: **Her self-confidence.**

Cleopatra's historical legacy as a sex object boils down to the fact that she would not be denied. She asked for what she wanted when she wanted it, and when she didn't get what she asked for, she looked somewhere else. When her brother kicked her out of the country, she assembled an entire *army* to take back her rightful place. When one vital political alliance died, she immediately hooked up with another. No matter how unfortunate the situation, Cleopatra never lacked in self-belief and always kept moving forward.

⇗ HEAT FACTOR: **Hot enough to melt more than one world leader (and also hot enough to burn the world down if things turned against her).**

We can't know for sure what Cleopatra really looked like, and there may have been debate about how attractive she was, but accounts of the time make it clear that there could be no debating her impact on other people. She was bold and seductive in equal measure, and she never failed to use whatever sex appeal she did have to her advantage. But that kind of confidence, while certainly sexy, can be problematic when the situation becomes desperate.

QUOTABLES

"She controlled virtually the entire Mediterranean coast, the last great kingdom of any Egyptian ruler. For a fleeting moment she held the fate of the Western world in her hands."

biographer Stacy Schiff

"Her actual beauty in itself was not so remarkable that none could be compared with her, or that no one could see her without being struck by it, but the contact of her presence . . . was irresistible. . . . The character that attended all she said or did, was something bewitching."

Plutarch

BENJAMIN FRANKLIN

"the first American"

VITAL STATS

YEARS: *1706 – 1790*

COUNTRY OF ORIGIN: *USA*

AREAS OF INFLUENCE: *Politics, Science, Literature*

STYLE OF SEDUCTION: *Droppin' knowledge*

№ 2

Benjamin Franklin was a man with his finger in every pie. He knew everyone, did everything, and made a difference everywhere. As a renowned scientist, politician, inventor, flirt, philanthropist, conversationalist, and writer, he left his mark.

⟿ FRANKLIN'S LIFE STORY

The fifteenth child of candle maker Josiah Franklin, Benjamin Franklin was the last-born son of two incredibly busy parents. At age fifteen, when his parents expected him to enter the church, young Benjamin instead began an apprenticeship at his brother James's printing press. While there, he cultivated his love of reading, writing, and subtly rebelling against pretty much every authority figure he came into contact with. As a result, he was not long for his brother's shop and soon took off for Philadelphia (an act for which, as an apprentice, he could have been arrested).

While in Philadelphia, Franklin occupied himself with various typesetting and bookkeeping jobs, but the itch to make an impact remained strong. By age twenty-one, he gathered some pals and started an organization for ambitious young people like himself eager for self-improvement. He called this community the Junto. It began as a kind of book club, but developed into a book-swapping system for books that were too expensive for any one member to own himself. Eventually this swapping system morphed into an actual lending library housed in what today is Independence Hall. (So give Ben Franklin a nod the next time you hear the phrase, "Having fun isn't hard when you have a library card.")

In 1743, Franklin founded the Academy and College of Philadelphia (later to become the University of Pennsylvania). This marked a major shift in his ambitions from the sciences and local affairs to public policy more generally. Later that same year, he formed the American Philosophical Society, which was intended as a place for scientists across the country to share ideas about their projects. Six years later, his incredible accolades in societal and technological work earned him a spot as Philadelphia's justice of the peace, cementing his transition into politics.

A rapid rise to the top of the political food chain found Ben Franklin in England in 1757, protesting the country's interference in political and religious freedom on behalf of the Pennsylvania Assembly. In 1764, Franklin was made speaker of the Pennsylvania House, and speak he did—

loudly. Beginning with the organization of a militia, he eventually got the hang of being a spy and specialized in covert action in a second mission to Great Britain just before the Revolutionary War.

The ambassador to Paris later referred to Franklin as a "veteran of mischief"—and can't you just picture him in an XL black trench coat with a fedora perched atop that curly white wig? When he returned to Pennsylvania, the Revolutionary War was in full swing. He made some revisions to the Declaration of Independence as one of the appointed Committee of Five, and his signature brought about eternal change to the nation we know today as the United States of America. In response to fellow committee member John Hancock's insistence that all five must remain of one mind, Franklin cheekily replied, "Yes, we must, indeed, all hang together, or most assuredly, we shall all hang separately." His résumé also eventually included such occupations as the first United States postmaster general, ambassador to France, and president of Pennsylvania.

➔ THE STORY OF HIS SEX LIFE

Ben Franklin's family life was not possessed of the remarkable polish (or virtue) of his political career. At age seventeen, he proposed to then fifteen-year-old Deborah Read. She turned him down and married another man, John Rogers, when Franklin moved to London. But after Rogers abandoned Read and Franklin returned to America, Franklin forgave and forgot and obtained a common law

YOUNG BEN FRANKLIN'S "THIRTEEN VIRTUES"

➔ **Temperance:** Eat not to dullness; drink not to elevation.

➔ **Silence:** Speak not but what may benefit others or yourself; avoid trifling conversations.

➔ **Order:** Let all your things have their places; let each part of your business have its time.

➔ **Resolution:** Resolve to perform what you ought; perform without fail what you resolve.

➔ **Frugality:** Make no expense but to do good to others or yourself; that is, waste nothing.

➔ **Industry:** Lose not time; be always employed in something useful; cut off all unnecessary actions.

➔ **Sincerity:** Use no hurtful deceit; think innocently and justly; speak accordingly.

➔ **Justice:** Wrong none by doing injuries or omitting the benefits that are your duty.

➔ **Moderation:** Avoid extremes; forbear resenting injuries so much as you think you deserve.

➔ **Cleanliness:** Tolerate no uncleanliness in body, clothes, or habitation.

➔ **Tranquility:** Be not disturbed at trifles or accidents common or unavoidable.

➔ **Chastity:** Rarely use venery but for health or offspring; never to dullness, weakness, or the injury of your own or another's peace or reputation.

➔ **Humility:** Imitate Jesus and Socrates.

marriage to Read, who in turn took in Franklin's illegitimate son. This son, William, was joined by a baby brother (who died soon after of smallpox) and a sister called Sally. Franklin is often thought of as a womanizer, and he did spend a lot of time away from home, but there's no convincing evidence that his flirtatious, charismatic manner amounted to a whole lot of real infidelity.

⇾ WHY HE MATTERS

Seriously? What ISN'T he known for? Statesman, optometrist, librarian, volunteer firefighter—Ben Franklin didn't just occupy these roles, he created them! He's best known for being one of the Founding Fathers, as well as one of the first abolitionists.

⇾ BEST FEATURE: **His total package-iness.**

We all recognize Ben Franklin today as the jolly and bespectacled old Santa Claus figure from portraits that were painted very late in his life, but as a young man he was physically fit and even considered becoming a swimming instructor at one point. When he wasn't swimming alongside ships, however, he charmed just about everyone around him with his wit, intelligence, and energy. His early scientific work was critical to the understanding of electricity, and among his inventions are the lightning rod, bifocals, meteorology, and

 the Franklin stove. As a young man, he abstained from meat so that he'd have more money for books, but even when he had money to spare and settled into a more beer-infused, conversational

lifestyle, his openness and confidence ensured that admirers were never far away.

⇾ HEAT FACTOR: **If you like America, you'll *love* Ben Franklin.**

Imagine a modern-day date with Ben Franklin: grab lunch at City Hall, maybe; invent a new alphabet; take an insider walking tour of Philly's historical sites; pass some bills; maybe grab some froyo; stop by the lab to make sure the experiments are going well, then radically change the world—all in a day's work. You might have to deal with always living in the shadow of the guy who was on the half dollar coin, but this seems to be one of the rare cases when being second fiddle isn't half bad.

QUOTABLES

"Never leave that till to-morrow which you can do to-day."

from *Poor Richard's Almanac*

"In reality there is, perhaps, no one of our natural passions so hard to subdue as pride . . . For even if I could conceive that I had completely overcome it, I should probably be proud of my humility."

At the signing of the Declaration of Independence, July 4, 1776

MARIE ANTOINETTE

"Madame Deficit"

N⁰ 3

The last queen of France got a reputation as a decadent snob who wasted her impoverished country's money on herself. Maybe she was just a selfish teenager who became queen too soon? Either way—spoiler alert—she ended up losing her head.

➔ ANTOINETTE'S LIFE STORY

Marie Antoinette was the fifteenth of the sixteen children of Emperor Francis I. When she was fifteen, she was married to Louis XVI of France. The young dauphin, or heir to the French throne, was one year her senior. When she arrived at the Palace of Versailles, the people adored the lively Austrian beauty. Four years later, Louis's father died and she became a teenage queen.

But times were tough in Marie's new kingdom. France was deeply in debt from the Seven Years' War and an unsuccessful harvest left the people of France starving. The new queen seemed oblivious to their struggles. While peasants starved in the streets, Marie Antoinette entertained lavishly, developed a penchant for gambling, ordered three hundred gowns every year of her rule, and built a new palace at Fontainebleu. To make matters worse, it took her eight years to bear a child (which happened to be a girl—not the royal family's preferred gender!), and eleven years of marriage to produce a son and heir. Her people began to turn against her. When the queen finally had

children, she spent weeks away at the royal retreat, Petit Trianon, usually without her husband. Pamphlets lambasting Antoinette for her reckless spending began circulating just as the country teetered on the edge of bankruptcy. Meanwhile, the National Assembly—a new organization that advocated for democratic rule—gained traction, potentially threatening the monarchy. When the French people stormed the Bastille on July 14, 1789—one of their most visible revolutionary acts—the queen found herself on the wrong side of history.

Soon after the incident at the Bastille, a mob of revolutionaries expelled the royal family from Versailles and forcibly relocated them to Paris. Marie Antoinette was eventually jailed, brought before the Revolutionary Tribunal, and beheaded by guillotine.

head on shoulders one last time

DIAMOND NECKLACE AFFAIR

One of Marie Antoinette's most memorable blunders wasn't actually her fault. Her friend, Cardinal de Rohan, was tricked into buying a $4.7 million diamond necklace for her highness because he read forged letters claiming that the queen was too embarrassed to ask Louis for such a lavish gift. When Marie Antoinette discovered the scheme and caught its perpetrator, she had a *V* for *voleuse*, or "thief," branded onto the woman's chest and threw her in jail. To add insult to injury, even though the queen wasn't involved in the scheme at all, the French people still treated her like a criminal who had greedily sought the necklace.

Marie Antoinette was rumored to have had many extramarital romances, including an affair with Axel von Fersen, a Swedish count. Shortly before her death, Fersen risked his life by sneaking into the royal palace just to be near her. Upon her death, he wrote, "Why, oh why did I not die for her on the twentieth of June?"

⟶ WHY SHE MATTERS

Marie Antoinette's most famous saying is "Let them eat cake." Although history tells us that she never actually uttered this phrase (it was in fact first expressed in Rousseau's *Confessions*, and the word that is now often translated as "cake" was really something more like "brioche"), her documented actions—like buying jewelry that cost as much as a house or trussing her hair up into elaborate bouffants—did a fair enough job of showing her utter disregard for the poor and their problems. She remains a symbol of a decadent monarchy, out of touch with the real world.

⟶ THE STORY OF HER SEX LIFE

It has been said that Louis XVI never kept a mistress—no small feat in the days when French kings typically had more than one. This is not to say the romance between Louis and Marie was idyllic—far from it. Marie's brother, Joseph, had to be dispatched to help the pair with their love-making when they had not produced an heir. He reported they were "two complete blunderers."

More gowns, please!

⟶ BEST FEATURE:
Her fashion sense.

There's something to be said for a lady who rocks new frocks—three hundred a year, in case you forgot— while the people screamed for her blood. Nearly every portrait of the queen attests to her glam style. Her eye for home decor wasn't bad, either: Hundreds of years after the end of the monarchy, Marie Antoinette's home at Versailles, filled with paintings, mirrors, and a whole lot of gold, remains a popular tourist destination.

⚜ HEAT FACTOR: **You'd better be ready to pay up if you're going to take Marie Antoinette out. This girl has expensive taste.**

Elaborately embroidered silk dresses and an impressive head of hair do little to make up for Marie's shocking unconcern for the common people. That said, it's not as if she was the only monarch who'd rather hang out in a palace than make sure that the people in her country weren't starving. She gets a consolation point to make up for being singled out by history.

MARIE ANTOINETTE SPLASHES INTO MODERN HOLLYWOOD

To many historians' (and some critics') dismay, Marie Antoinette's life story—and her perceived ethos—were given the twenty-first-century treatment in a 2006 film starring Kirsten Dunst. Released by Columbia Pictures and written and directed by the provocative and always newsworthy Sofia Coppola, the hyperstylized film earned an Academy Award for Best Costume Design. In an effort to update the period piece, the soundtrack was littered with electro and postpunk buzz bands, and Converse sneakers even made a cameo alongside all the historical hairdos. Marie Antoinette is just timeless like that.

IN HER OWN WORDS

"I put on my rouge and wash my hands in front of the whole world."

"I am terrified of being bored."

To a German official: *"Speak French, Monsieur. From now on I hear no language other than French."*

On the way to the guillotine: *"Courage? The moment when my ills are going to end is not the moment when courage is going to fail me."*

LORD BYRON

"mad, bad, and dangerous to know"

VITAL STATS

YEARS: *1788 – 1824*

COUNTRY OF ORIGIN: *England*

AREAS OF INFLUENCE:
Literature, Culture

STYLE OF SEDUCTION:
Breakin' hearts

W hile many poets of the romantic era weren't actually all that romantic, British poet Lord Byron was known both for his own epic passions and for the romantic heroes he created on the page.

→ BYRON'S LIFE STORY

As a child, Byron had the nickname *le diable boiteux*, or "the limping devil"—a reference to his clubfoot. His affliction made him deeply self-conscious, but it didn't slow him down: He refused to wear a brace and still managed to excel at sports as a boy. His character at the time was described as "courageous, quarrelsome, resentful, sensitive, abounding in animal spirits . . . full of mischief."

For a university education, Byron headed to Trinity College, Cambridge, where his free spirit chafed under the strict Anglican morality. While a student, Byron achieved some notoriety with his first book of poetry, *Fugitive Pieces*, but the book was not a financial success, and he left university in crippling debt. In spite of his dire financial straits, he embarked on his "Grand Tour" of Europe, a trans-European trip taken by noble youth of the time. Unfortunately, due to financial difficulties and the Napoleonic wars, the trip had to be rerouted and he missed some of the traditional Grand Tour destinations in Europe. Byron instead explored Greece, Albania, and Constantinople.

Upon returning to England, Byron delivered a number of passionate speeches as a member of the House of Lords, branding himself an extremist in his views on religion and social reform. He soon left England again, this time for Italy, by way of Switzerland. In Switzerland he spent time with author Mary Shelley and her family. Both authors shared and compared their work, and one of the products of this time in Geneva became Shelley's famous *Frankenstein*.

When he settled in Italy, Byron published the first two cantos of *Don Juan*, an epic poem, in 1819. *Don Juan* recounts the exploits of a famous womanizer, and it remains Byron's best-known and most admired work. Fellow author Goethe called it "a work of boundless genius," but it was also criticized for its apparent immorality.

In addition to producing great literature, Byron was also a political activist. He aided in the Italian fight for independence from Austria, and later followed his political convictions to Greece as well, which was then in the midst of a massive struggle for independence. In an effort to aid the

Greek resistance, Byron chartered the sailing ship *Hercules* and began giving orders to a rebel army to attack a Turkish-held fortress. Sadly he developed a feverish sickness and died before the mission could begin.

⇨ THE STORY OF HIS SEX LIFE

Byron married Annabella Milbanke in 1815 but carried on numerous extramarital affairs over the course of his lifetime with both men and women. In addition to the child he had with his wife (Ada Lovelace, who grew up to be a famous mathematician; see page 36), he fathered at least one other illegitimate child, and possibly many more. Furthermore, he is thought to have had an incestuous relationship with his half-sister, Augusta, who may have borne him another child. Most famous of his many paramours, however, was Lady Caroline Lamb, who notoriously called him "mad, bad, and dangerous to know."

⇨ WHY HE MATTERS

Byron was the foremost literary celebrity of his day and remains widely read even now, but his influence was nowhere more important than in overcoming—or at least lessening—many cultural taboos of the time. Throughout his hugely successful career as a poet, Byron consistently shocked Victorian audiences with his frank and graphic portrayal of sexuality and sexual acts. The writer offered no apologies and only occasionally censored his own pieces for the sake of profit.

BYRON'S ANIMAL ADDICTION

Lord Byron was a lifelong animal lover, and wherever he went he had animals in tow. It sounds charming, but you can imagine how it could present some problems for those who had the misfortune to host the notorious Lord. Here is just a sampling of some of his most famous companions.

⇨ **A Tamed Bear.** While attending Trinity College, Byron adopted a tamed bear and housed it in his dormitory room.

⇨ **A Wolf Dog.** When he left university and moved to Newstead Abbey (tamed bear in tow), he found a new companion as well: a dog that was part wolf.

⇨ **Geese.** It's said that when Lord Byron learned that the three geese strapped in his coach to Genoa were to be slaughtered and eaten, he covertly rescued them. Uncharacteristically, however, he did not wish to keep the wild birds, and instead gave them as a gift to his banker.

⇨ **A Menagerie.** While embarking on an affair with Theresa Guiccioli, Byron kept ten horses, eight dogs, three monkeys, five cats, an eagle, a crow, and a falcon at his villa.

As recently as 1969, a memorial for Lord Byron was placed in the Poets' Corner in Westminster Abbey. Aside from being one of the most prolific poets of the romantic period, Byron created the figure of the Byronic hero—a trope still used in poetry as a symbol of someone of high class but little tact, irresponsible, self-destructive, and yet possessed of an unceasing zest for life and love.

➔ BEST FEATURE: **His unique personality.**
Lord Byron is sometimes considered the first public celebrity. As a result of his fame, Byron pushed the limits—even wearing curling papers (the Victorian equivalent of hot rollers) to bed each night to style his hair. In addition to pushing the limits of fashion, he also played with the boundaries of art and sexuality, challenging his contemporaries' views of what was acceptable.

➔ HEAT FACTOR: **Byron was a man of means who knew his way around the thesaurus . . . and the bedroom.**

Lord Byron was the archetype of the sexy, tortured poet. His adventurous sexuality, paired with serious athleticism in the physical prime of his early life, made him an attractive figure, in spite of his philandering. On the upside of his Casanova lifestyle, Byron's embrace of many forms of sexual expression (minus the alleged incest) was ahead of its time and helped to set the stage for more progressive thinking on sexuality in the years to come.

QUOTABLES

"Friendship is Love without his wings!"

Lord Byron, *Hours of Idleness*

"My great comfort is, that the temporary celebrity I have wrung from the world has been in the very teeth of all opinions and prejudices. I have flattered no ruling powers; I have never concealed a single thought that tempted me."

Lord Byron, letter to Thomas Moore, 1814

"The world is rid of Lord Byron, but the deadly slime of his touch still remains."

John Constable, letter to the Rev. John Fisher, 1824

GEORGE SAND

VITAL STATS

YEARS: *1804 – 1876*

COUNTRY OF ORIGIN: *France*

AREA OF INFLUENCE:
Literature, Politics

STYLE OF SEDUCTION:
Bendin' genders

№ 5

George Sand was a bisexual, cross-dressing literary super-star who took no prisoners in shaping politics, bucking conventions, and generally mixing it up. Her friends and lovers constitute a who's who of nineteenth-century Europe. She was a queen among men and a king among women.

→ SAND'S LIFE STORY

George Sand was a polarizing figure across Europe, and opinions about her among her contemporaries are stunningly varied. Ivan Turgenev, for instance, called her a "brave man," whereas Alfred de Musset praised her as a "womanly woman." She was born Amantine Lucile Aurore in 1804, to the Dupin family in Paris, France, and prior to changing her name, Amantine was for the most part raised by her grandmother at the countryside estate of Nohant. It would have been a fairly conventional aristocratic childhood, but there was an element of rebellion and scandal present as well, since Amantine's father, an illegitimate son of nobility, unapologetically married a lower-class woman. That fact would play a pivotal role in her politics as an adult.

After a brief stint at a convent, Amantine married Baron Casimir Dudevant in 1822. She then gave birth to two children, a son named Maurice and a daughter named Solange. The marriage was not destined to last, however, and after  nine years Sand left her husband to move to Paris with her children in tow.

Although she was still officially married to Dudevant, Amantine struck up a friendship (which later became more than a friendship) with the novelist Jules Sandeau. The pair worked together under the name "Jules Sand"—a pseudonym that allowed the provocative young woman to see her work in *Le Figaro*. The name also eventually inspired her own authorial moniker, George Sand. Though Sandeau and Sand eventually split, the groundwork had been laid for Sand to embark on her own literary career. In 1832, Sand wrote *Indiana*, the first of three novels that would give voice to her strong conviction that the only way to be a truly attractive woman would be to combine a beautiful face with a beautiful mind. The ability to think for oneself was essential.

In addition to attacking conventional standards about femininity and morality in print, she provoked the public with the way she lived her life. After changing her name, Sand dressed in men's trousers (complemented by the occasional top

hat) and made her rounds in the bookish Paris circuit with tobacco always close at hand—a serious no-no for women associated with the French nobility.

In 1838, Sand took her children with her to the island of Majorca to spend several months with romantic composer and pianist Frédéric Chopin. She wrote about their famous affair in the 1855 publication *Un Hiver à Majorque*. Chopin's existing tuberculosis went from bad to worse in the winter chill, and Sand eventually went from lover to caretaker. After a decade, the duo parted ways. Her son, Maurice, sided with Sand, while Solange outraged her mother by remaining supportive of Chopin. Sand did not attend Chopin's funeral in 1848.

Sand continued to write novels about class inequality, hitting her stride with a stretch of rustic and pastoral novels in the late 1840s and 1850s and penning her autobiography, *Histoire de ma vie*, in 1855. In 1873, she completed the final work, *Contes d'une grand'mère*, written for her grandchildren. It was the last of the fifty-five books she would write before her death in 1876. She was buried at her home in Nohant.

✦ THE STORY OF HER SEX LIFE

Despite, and very possibly because of, her headstrong denial of social norms, Sand caught the eye of at least nine impassioned writers, artists, and politicians between 1831 and 1847. Among these were such luminaries as playwright Prosper Mérimée, the aforementioned composer Frédéric Chopin, and actress Marie Dorval. It's hard not to look at pictures of Sand without getting a sense of why both men and women fell hard for her: Her confidence is undeniable. Endlessly pursuing her artistic ambition, Sand wrote with a tirelessness that put other authors of her era to shame. Her published correspondence with a number of admirers makes for bewitching extracurricular reading.

✦ WHY SHE MATTERS

George Sand spent her entire adult life fighting for the rights of women, riling up the working class, and shocking all of Europe with her freewheeling lifestyle. In addition to being a fierce feminist before there was really a feminist movement to speak of, she was also a popular novelist and rabble-rouser who still found the time to carry on lusty affairs *and* be a great mother to her kids. She matters because she *wasn't* (EVER) what people expected her to be.

✦ BEST FEATURE: **Androgyny.**

Sand's penchant for superchic cross-dressing made her an appropriate paramour for men and women alike. Alfred de Musset, one of her earliest writer flings, published the spicy 1833 novel *Gamiani*, or *Two Nights of Excess*, based on Sand's relationship with the actress Marie Dorval. In the face of nineteenth-century French society's condemnation of same-sex affairs and women's independence, Sand laughed and lived her life exactly as she wished.

⌖ HEAT FACTOR: **Scandalously hot.**

Seemingly oblivious to the standard for female behavior in an upper-class setting, Sand relied entirely on her intellect and wit to exercise her sensuality. No stranger to criticism, she found ways to circumvent the system while igniting the hearts of some of Paris's most influential and productive minds. In this case, crush-worthy is an understatement; Sand was a heartbreaker and a soul shaker. She was the complete package—appropriating masculinity without renouncing her own seductive nature, acting bullheaded in public while still ensuring the safety of her children in private, and staying true to her convictions even when offered an easy (and lucrative) out.

QUOTABLES

"What a repulsive woman Sand is! But is she really a woman? I am inclined to doubt it."

Frédéric Chopin

"Her ideas on morals have the same depth of judgment and delicacy of feeling as those of janitresses and kept women. . . . The fact that there are men who could become enamoured of this slut is indeed a proof of the abasement of the men of this generation."

Charles Baudelaire

"You've gone and become George Sand; otherwise, you would merely have been Madame so and so, scribbling away."

Alfred de Musset

"At her funeral I cried like an ass."

Gustave Flaubert

HARRIET BEECHER STOWE

"the little woman who made this great war"

VITAL STATS

YEARS: *1811 – 1896*

COUNTRY OF ORIGIN: *USA*

AREA OF INFLUENCE: *Literature*

STYLE OF SEDUCTION:
Stirrin' up emotions

№ 6

As a novelist and an activist, Harriet Beecher Stowe changed the world. Her abolitionist tome, *Uncle Tom's Cabin*, popularized the antislavery movement, while her civil rights activism helped abolish slavery once and for all.

⇝ STOWE'S LIFE STORY

Harriet Beecher Stowe was one of eleven children born to prominent Presbyterian minister Lyman Beecher and his wife, Roxanna (who died when Harriet was five years old). The family was deeply religious: All seven of Harriet's brothers went on to become ministers, and her oldest sister, Catharine, founded a seminary for girls, where Harriet was first a student and then a teacher.

Stowe began writing shortly after her mother's death. Her first contribution to the world of letters was an epitaph for a dead kitten. Receiving an education that was generally reserved  for young men, the teenage schoolteacher spent many hours composing essays. When she was twenty-one, her family relocated to Ohio when her father accepted an appointment at a seminary there. Shortly after the move, she met theology professor Calvin Stowe, and they were married. She kept up her writing, publishing a children's primer and a collection of short stories within the next few years.

Harriet and Calvin, both passionate abolitionists, lived just across the river from Kentucky and could hardly ignore its thriving slave trade. Stowe befriended fellow abolitionists who were involved in the Underground Railroad, a system of safe houses that helped fugitive slaves escape to freedom. She spent countless hours speaking with the escapees and collecting slave narratives. These narratives became the inspiration for her first novel, *Uncle Tom's Cabin*, which was initially published in installments in an abolitionist magazine, *The National Era*, in 1851. In 1852, she published the full manuscript as a novel, and with the publication of her book, the American reckoning with slavery continued to develop.

Stowe's sentimental depiction of long-suffering slaves took the world by storm, becoming a best seller almost instantly. Stowe quickly gained celebrity status, using her platform to speak out against the evils of slavery. As legend has it, when she met then President Abraham Lincoln, he asked, "Is this the little woman who made this great war?" Stowe would go on to write many more books, plays, hymns, short stories, and poems before her death at age eighty-five, but none of these works impacted the United States quite like *Uncle Tom's Cabin*.

NOOK FARM

Located on the outer edge of Hartford, Connecticut, Stowe's large family home was part of Nook Farm, a neighborhood designed to attract politically minded writers and artists. It became an intellectual hotspot where many creative types took up residence.

In fact, one of Stowe's closest friends was Samuel Clemens—better known as Mark Twain. She gave him a lesson in proper conduct, however, when he showed up to her home with no hat and tie. Not one to stand for even mild disrespect, she called him out, and he had his butler promptly bring the accessories on a tray. Stowe joked that she'd settle for his visits in installments.

→ THE STORY OF HER SEX LIFE

The long marriage of Calvin and Harriet Beecher Stowe was defined by mutual respect and strong values. Calvin encouraged

Calvin and Harriet

Harriet's writing endeavors, having once told her she "must be a literary woman." Indeed, Harriet's literary output dwarfed that of her husband. Her paychecks did the same—her considerable author's royalties enabled the couple to buy a Connecticut mansion and a winter home in Florida. Their relationship wasn't entirely rosy, however, and they did have to endure real tragedies: Of their seven children, only three would outlive their parents.

→ WHY SHE MATTERS

Although *Uncle Tom's Cabin* was an international chart-topper and permanent fixture on school reading lists, its literary merits and political views were questioned from the outset. Stowe's more radical contemporaries criticized the book because it didn't call for an immediate end to slavery. Some modern critics hold the book accountable for creating negative African American stereotypes. Stowe, a dedicated abolitionist, would likely have been horrified by these accusations. Despite these detractions, her personal legacy remains relatively untarnished, and most historians can at least agree that *Uncle Tom's Cabin* launched a wave of social change that made America a better place.

⇒ BEST FEATURE: **Her dedication.**

In addition to being a prolific author and unwavering activist, Harriet Beecher Stowe also managed to raise seven children and foster an equal partnership with her husband. Pretty impressive in an era when women rarely worked outside the home. "Never give up then, for that is just the place and time that the tide will turn," she once said. She followed her own advice and changed the world because of it.

⇒ HEAT FACTOR: **Buttoned-up, but still burning with a desire for change.**

Stowe, a deeply religious woman with a strong moral compass, wrote a very long, very sentimental novel that inspired people to change their political beliefs. That being said, the writer and critic James Baldwin famously hated *Uncle Tom's Cabin* because its protagonist was too saintly—and too asexual—to pass as a real person. So in his view, the book failed to reckon with the reality of black Americans, despite the fact that the book did help to achieve real change.

QUOTABLES

"Her lever was the wand of art, her fulcrum was the human heart."
poet Oliver Wendell Holmes Sr.

"When I entered the White House, I was not a Christian. Now I am a Christian."
Abraham Lincoln to Stowe, citing her influence

"Uncle Tom's Cabin came from the heart rather than the head. It was an outburst of deep feeling, a cry in the darkness. The writer no more thought of style or literary excellence than the mother who rushes into the street and cries for help to save her children from a burning house thinks of the teachings of the rhetorician or the elocutionist."
son Charles Stowe

ADA LOVELACE

"an enchantress of numbers"

VITAL STATS

YEARS: *1815 – 1852*

COUNTRY OF ORIGIN: *England*

AREAS OF INFLUENCE:
Mathematics, Computer Science

STYLE OF SEDUCTION:
Talkin' nerdy

№ 7

Ada Lovelace was Lord Byron's only legitimate daughter and is recognized and honored today as the first computer programmer. (She was also, like her father, unafraid to borrow some money in pursuit of love and pleasure.)

→ LOVELACE'S LIFE STORY

When she was just five weeks old, Ada Lovelace was placed in the care of her grandmother, Lady Byron. The cause of this quasi adoption? The fact that her parents' marriage was very much on the rocks. (It was, perhaps more accurately, on the boulders.) Lord Byron was a lifelong philanderer (see page 24 on Lord Byron for more on that) and divorced from Ada's mother, Baroness Byron, shortly after she had given birth. As a result of this sequence of events, Baroness Byron wanted to have as little to do with her daughter as possible— only insisting that she study math and science rather than literature.

To ensure she did not inherit her father's supposed madness, the young girl was educated by the best of Europe's academics, including radical activist William Frend. Upon turning seventeen, Ada began hitting the town. At one high society party, Ada's mentor, Mary Somerville, introduced her to Charles Babbage, the man now generally recognized as the father of the computer.

Small talk at the soiree revolved around Babbage's newfangled idea for a number-crunching machine, called the "Analytical Engine." Enraptured by the possibilities she saw in this machine, Ada got her hands on Luigi Menabrea's notes on the idea (in Italian) and sent her own translation to Babbage. Whether influenced by her aristocratic standing or her synthesis of these ideas, he requested her thoughts on the concept as well. Her notes were extensive—much longer than the original summary. It was Babbage who, upon reading her work, pronounced Lady Lovelace an "enchantress of numbers."

In these notes lay the first algorithm intended for use not by a human but by a machine. Though scholarly debate still rages about whether Ada truly wrote the algorithm independently or relied on calculations Babbage had already written, the fact remains that she was listed as an author. Even more impressively, she was the first to predict the potential for the Analytical Machine's more sophisticated service as a tool for graphic design or music. Sadly, the story ends there, since Ada's work lay dormant for more than a hundred years until our modern-day mathematicians had a chance to catch up. Her early death, at just age thirty-seven, to cancer was preceded by an addiction to gambling, which found her in over £2,000 of debt at the end of her life.

➔ THE STORY OF HER SEX LIFE

With a last name like Lovelace, it's no surprise that this brainy beauty found some time for romance. (We'd need a sophisticated equation just for tallying up the names in her little black book.) She had a thing for smart suitors from an early age and at one point even tried to run away with her tutor. However, like most teenage vagrants, she was caught. This, of course, put quite a damper on her social life, as her grandmother, Lady Byron, doubled down on the discipline and replaced the cute tutor with a more serious scholar. Lucky for us, Ada fell hard for her studies at this point in her life, and she used the opportunity to maximize her understanding of all things numerical.

Unsurprisingly, her books could only distract her for so long. And in 1835, she revealed that she was in a relationship with one William King. Before long the two were married, and before longer they had three children. Like her mother

before her, Ada had little interest in rearing the three new arrivals and, therefore, opted out of the whole "mothering" thing to focus on advanced math studies instead. This left King with day-care duty, but he supported nearly all of Ada's pursuits, and adopted the progressive Mr. Mom role like a champ. It should be noted that Lady Byron lent a hand as well.

Just five years later, the rumor mill began to churn afresh with talk of Ada's rather intense relationships with male colleagues and friends. Whether justified or not, King destroyed over one hundred letters from such companions.

➔ WHY SHE MATTERS

Over a century before the invention of the World Wide Web, this countess paved the way for the likes of Bill Gates and Mark Zuckerberg as the first computer programmer—though the machine was never actually built. In the twenty-first century, several of the most powerful and profitable companies in the world—Apple, Google, and Microsoft, just to name a few—are run by executives who got their start as computer programmers. Steve Jobs's iPhone legacy would never have been possible without Ada's original algorithm, which has become the foundation for the wealth of programming languages that enable our world to access limitless information with just a click of a button. In pre-programmer times, she considered herself an analyst and metaphysician, lacking the language to categorize herself as anything more than an academic. In 1979, the United States Department of Defense named a software language "Ada" to honor her contributions to computer science.

⇢ BEST FEATURE: **Her brains.**

Ada Lovelace is a stunning example of a strong and capable woman breaking into a field that was—and remains—dominated by men. Ada certainly had presence, with her huge updos and elaborate floral dresses (which by no means flat-tered her figure, but who cares?). But it was her stunning intellect that kept all those bright young gentlemen coming back for more.

⇢ HEAT FACTOR: **Smart enough to know what would be hot two centuries later.**

There's nothing hotter than algorithms right now. They're the engines that power the internet—and Lovelace was there at the beginning. She was one of the few people who could see how powerful this tool could become.

IN HER OWN WORDS

"I never am really satisfied that I understand anything; because, understand it well as I may, my comprehension can only be an infinitesimal fraction of all I want to understand about the many connections and relations which occur to me, how the matter in question was first thought of or arrived at, etc., etc."

"We may say most aptly, that the Analytical Engine weaves algebraical patterns just as the Jacquard-loom weaves flowers and leaves."

"The Analytical Engine has no pretensions whatever to originate anything. It can do whatever we know how to order it to perform. It can follow analysis, but it has no power of anticipating any analytical revelations or truths. Its province is to assist us in making available what we are already acquainted with."

FREDERICK DOUGLASS

"There's a better day coming."

VITAL STATS

YEARS: *1818 – 1895*

COUNTRY OF ORIGIN: *USA*

AREA OF INFLUENCE:
Civil Rights

STYLE OF SEDUCTION:
*Passionate activism
and oratory*

№ 8

One of America's most celebrated orators escaped slavery to become a groundbreaking author and publisher, an important abolitionist, and a tireless supporter of equal human rights for all.

→ DOUGLASS'S LIFE STORY

Frederick Douglass was born into slavery as Frederick Augustus Washington Bailey. As a boy, he was sold to a Maryland plantation and eventually sent to serve a couple, the Aulds, in their Baltimore home. Sophia Auld began teaching Douglass to read, but her husband put the kibosh on the tutelage, as slave owners at the time were often concerned that educated slaves would be more likely to resist their subjugation. There are echoes of this same sentiment—albeit from a different and much healthier perspective—in one of Douglass's more famous sayings: "Knowledge is the pathway from slavery to freedom."

Once Douglass had tasted literacy, he couldn't be stopped. He scored reading lessons from white children in the neighborhood, and when their lessons ended, he continued learning on his own.

When he was eventually hired out to a plantation owner, he taught his fellow slaves how to read as well. As a teenager, he tried and failed to escape on two separate occasions; then,

at roughly twenty years of age, he collaborated with his future wife on the plan that finally took them to freedom in the North. When there, he changed his name, got married to his beloved Anna Murray, and began his heroic efforts to put an end to slavery.

He started small. At first, he spoke about his experiences in church and abolitionist meetings. He began reading William Lloyd Garrison's publication, *The Liberator.* Garrison was blown away by Douglass's powerful speech at an antislavery meeting and encouraged his efforts as an orator. It was also Garrison who, in all likelihood, inspired Douglass to start his own abolitionist newspaper, *The North Star.* In 1845, he published the first version of his autobiography, then called *Narrative of the Life of Frederick Douglass, an American Slave*, which became an instant bestseller and brought him international acclaim. For the next two years, he toured Ireland and England, speaking out against slavery to packed meetinghouses.

By the time of the Civil War, Douglass's renown had grown large enough to capture the attention of President Lincoln. Lincoln discussed the treatment of African American soldiers with Douglass, and when the Union won the war and Lincoln abolished slavery, Douglass rejoiced, writing an enduring and influential speech encouraging former slaves to become "Self Made Men."

In the years that followed, Douglass broadened the focus of his activism to include fighting for the rights of women and other persecuted groups. His intellectual acumen and personal charisma gained popular and political acclaim: He would go on to work with Presidents Grant, Hayes, and Garfield. He published his last book, *The Life and Times of Frederick Douglass*, three years before his death in 1895.

⇸ The Story of His Sex Life

Shortly after Douglass and Anna Murray escaped to freedom, they were wed in New York City. Douglass put their five children to work as pint-sized abolitionists, helping him with his publications. According to his memoirs, he delighted in married life. After Murray's death, Douglass married Helen Pitts, who was nearly twenty years his junior. This was a man who couldn't afford a scandal (and his many enemies at that time were all too eager to discredit him); but luckily, he never had one.

⇸ Why He Matters

Through determination, luck, and the willful disregard of an entire system of oppression, Frederick Douglass learned to read, write, and change American history forever. His literacy alone made him an oddity in an age where the majority of black Americans never received any significant schooling. His unique skill set and his inimitable passion made him famous and gained him access to the political system. Douglass was born into an American nightmare and yet somehow set the template for the American dream. With less than bootstraps to begin with, he pulled himself up to a point where he was able to drastically improve the lives of millions of other Americans.

⇸ Best Feature: **His way with words.**

If Frederick Douglass could convince deeply racist politicians that black slaves should have the same rights as other Americans, just imagine what he would say on a date. His style was pretty great, too: His professional life called for him to dress in crisp and classic suits, but he let loose a little in his later years, growing a full head of bushy white hair and a complementary, fluffy beard.

fluffy beard

⇡ HEAT FACTOR: **Words come up short when confronted with Douglass's level of intelligence, attractiveness, resilience, and human decency.**

Frederick Douglass was the total package. At a time when racism was explicit, profound, and unrelenting, he fought for change. He was fighting a noble fight if ever there was one, and he not only made his case but also made friends almost everywhere he went. He was not to be denied.

QUOTABLES

"Flinty hearts were pierced, and cold ones melted by his eloquence."

a correspondent, upon hearing Douglass's speech at the 1841 Massachusetts Anti-Slavery Society convention

"At one time Mr. Douglass was travelling in the state of Pennsylvania, and was forced, on account of his colour, to ride in the baggage-car, in spite of the fact that he had paid the same price for his passage that the other passengers had paid. When some of the white passengers went into the baggage-car to console Mr. Douglass, and one of them said to him: 'I am sorry, Mr. Douglass, that you have been degraded in this manner,' Mr. Douglass straightened himself up on the box upon which he was sitting and replied: 'They cannot degrade Frederick Douglass. The soul that is within me no man can degrade. I am not the one that is being degraded on account of this treatment, but those who are inflicting it upon me.'"

Booker T. Washington

"In spite of law and gospel, despite of statues which thralled him and opportunities which jeered at him, he made himself by trampling on the law and breaking through the thick darkness that encompassed him."

Rochester Democrat and Chronicle, 1879

WILD BILL HICKOK

the original
Lone Ranger

VITAL STATS

YEARS: *1837 – 1876*

COUNTRY OF ORIGIN: *USA*

AREA OF INFLUENCE:
Public Safety

STYLE OF SEDUCTION:
Bad boy with a heart of gold

№ 9

You don't get the nickname Wild Bill by being everyone's best friend. Hickok may have been a dedicated abolitionist, sheriff, and Union soldier, but he still couldn't keep his temper in check with a pistol in his hand.

⇾ HICKOK'S LIFE STORY

James Butler Hickok grew up in Illinois, working as a farmhand by day and a liberator by night, helping his abolitionist father assist fugitive slaves in their escape to freedom. In his late teens, he moved to Kansas, the Wheat State, where he continued his antislavery efforts, served as a village constable, and got a reputation as a wild man when he killed a Teamster in a gunfight.

During the Civil War, Hickok worked for the Union Army, first as a wagon master and then as a military police officer, investigating counterfeiters, busting horse thieves, and hunting down soldiers who hadn't shown up for duty. His cunning caught the attention of General John Sandborn, who appointed him as his personal scout and spy. It was then that Hickok's signature brand of wily daring earned him the nickname Wild Bill.

UPSTANDING . . .

Hickok's reputation as a formidable lawman grew after the war, thanks in no small part to an overbaked profile in *Harper's* magazine that stated, among other things,

that he had killed ten men at once. He traveled around the West occupying various positions in law enforcement and racking up his body count

AND TERRIFYING!

to at least seven (though the press put the number much higher), including, in one sad instance, a friend whom he had unintentionally shot. The press reported on his every move, helping to upgrade his reputation from formidable lawman to Wild West icon.

Perhaps he was tired of all the shooting and bloodshed—or perhaps he discovered he liked attention more than justice—but in either case, Hickok abandoned law enforcement in favor of a career in show business. He attempted to host his own Wild West show, and when that proved unpopular, he performed with Buffalo Bill's shooting and rough riding revue instead.

As Wild Bill aged, he began to exhibit symptoms of a mystery disease that didn't seem to be treatable. Modern-day doctors have speculated that it could have been anything from gonorrhea to ophthalmia, which is an eye condition resulting in inflammation. The most likely diagnosis, though, is glaucoma, another eye condition that eventually causes the patient to go blind without proper treatment. Of course, Hickok was not the responsible type, and he would suffer from what were essentially blackouts from time to time. All the more remarkable is that even with what would now likely be considered legal blindness, he was one of best shots in town.

Nearing the age of forty, Wild Bill married a widow but soon abandoned her to head back out west and make his fortune in the boomtown of Deadwood. Instead of panning for gold, he spent his time gambling and was shot during a poker game. He was buried in South Dakota outside Deadwood.

⇥ THE STORY OF HIS SEX LIFE

Although Hickok's only marriage was brief and unremarkable, his legendary—if unconfirmed—relationship with Martha Jane Cannary was anything but. Cannary was the perfect partner for a fearsome frontiersman: She rode horses, shot guns, and drank (and cussed) like a man of the time.

the female Mr. Hickok

For these talents, she acquired the nickname Calamity Jane. The pair met at Fort Laramie in Wyoming and embarked together on the long ride to Deadwood in the Dakota Territory. Although Calamity Jane's memoirs discuss Hickok only briefly, and only as a friend, the pair are buried side by side.

DUCK BILL HICKOK

Hickok endured quite a few playground nicknames before adopting the effortlessly cool moniker Wild Bill, a reference that finally stuck. The earliest reports have him down as "Duck Bill," which some historians believed was a nod to his big ol' schnoz. This has been refuted by others, though, who claim that his nose actually appears hooked in photos. (You can judge for yourself!) Later on, he was sometimes called "Dutch Bill," though the origins of this are not clear. The best guess researchers have is that "Dutch Bill" was also a nod to his appearance. (Seems like a fair guess. That, or he always only paid for himself when out on dates?)

⇥ WHY HE MATTERS

The idea of the Wild West cowboy wouldn't loom as large or vivid in the American imagination without Wild Bill Hickok and his true grit. Poker wouldn't be the same, either: the Dead Man's Hand, a two-pair hand of black eights and aces, is named for the cards he was holding upon his death.

⇨ BEST FEATURE: **His roguish charm.**
There are few who can resist a fearless cowboy, especially one who used his wits and bravery to further the cause of good. (Usually.)

⇨ HEAT FACTOR: **Well, spending a night under the stars with Wild Bill would be anything but boring.**

Hickok's charisma was such that he remains a compelling figure one hundred and fifty years after his death (see: HBO's *Deadwood*). Cowboys are cool and everything, but Wild Bill's appeal has some limitations, namely his temper, the murder of innocents, and the fact that he probably smelled like a horse.

MURDER OF DAVID TUTT

Former Confederate soldier David Tutt was the perfect sidekick for Wild Bill, as they shared an interest in both gambling and guns. As the story goes, the two came to a disagreement over a gambling debt: Tutt won Hickok's treasured watch, Hickok asked Tutt not to wear it in public, and Tutt told him to get over it. Hickok told Tutt that if he ever saw him wearing the watch he'd shoot him, and that's exactly what happened. The morning after he'd won the watch, Tutt put it on, ran into Wild Bill, and was shot through the heart. Hickok avoided being convicted of murder because some witnesses testified that Tutt had fired the first shot.

QUOTABLES

"Wild Bill was a strange character, add to this figure a costume blending the immaculate neatness of the dandy with the extravagant taste and style of a frontiersman, you have Wild Bill, the most famous scout on the Plains."
General George Custer

"He's a very nice man. Big, I mean bigger than life."
The Rawhide Kid, Marvel Comics character

"Wild Bill, J.B. Hickok killed by the assassin Jack McCall in Deadwood Black Hills, August 2nd, 1876. Pard, we will meet again in the happy hunting ground to part no more. Good Bye, Colorado Charlie, C.H. Utter."
inscription on Hickok's grave marker

JOHN WILKES BOOTH

"I am abandoned."

VITAL STATS

YEARS: *1838 – 1865*
COUNTRY OF ORIGIN: *USA*
AREA OF INFLUENCE: *Politics*
STYLE OF SEDUCTION:
Playin' you false

№ 10

John Wilkes Booth was a moderately successful Shakespearean actor in the 1850s and '60s whose name lives on as a result of his infamous assassination of America's most beloved president: Abraham Lincoln. He was a seriously handsome devil and a seriously devilish dude.

✦ BOOTH'S LIFE STORY

John Wilkes Booth was born into an acting family, but from an early age, he was desperate to set himself apart. (This would prove to be difficult, despite some level of natural talent.) He was raised, along with his nine brothers and sisters, on a farm in Bel Air—not the paradise portrayed in *The Fresh Prince*, but rather a suburb of Baltimore. The Booth's summer home, however, showed how influential the family had become through their stagecraft. The estate was called Tudor Hall and sold in 1999 for almost half a million dollars. Both John and his brother Edwin (a fellow thespian) were born out of wedlock, and even though their father, Junius Brutus Booth, eventually married his mistress and John's mother, Mary Ann Holmes, both brothers probably would have endured a significant amount of public shaming.

Booth first made a name for himself as a teenager in his onstage debut in *Richard III* at a Baltimore theater. He quickly turned his rave reviews into a thriving career that took him around the country playing a variety of Shakespearean roles. The only downside of this was that his skills were constantly pitted against and compared to those of his brother, Edwin. Still, it was a successful career, and at his peak, John Wilkes Booth earned an annual salary of $20,000 per year—approximately sixty-six times what the average family earned annually at that time.

In the midst of his acting career, the eventual assassin decided to apply his zeal to a new endeavor as well: politics. A radical libertarian, Booth first joined what was referred to as the Know-Nothing Party, an organization dedicated to mitigating the number of Irish and German immigrants moving to the United States. Along with other conservatives, he came to believe that Lincoln's ultimate goal was to become king of America. In 1859, Booth demonstrated his aggres-

sive support of slavery by aiding in the capture of John Brown, an abolitionist who had led a major slave revolt. This action was a gateway to Booth's time as a secret agent for the Confederate Army during the Civil War.

In 1864, Booth began to develop more conventional criminal plans: He wanted to kidnap President Lincoln and bring him to Richmond, Virginia, where he could be ransomed for Confederate soldiers. Several cronies were drafted into the plot, including Lewis Powell, George Atzerodt, David Herold, Samuel Arnold, Michael O'Laughlen, and John Surratt. Booth put aside acting and reallocated his personal funds in order to purchase supplies for the developing kidnapping plot. But due to the financial expense and lack of concerted organization, coconspirators soon began dropping from the effort left and right.

Perhaps pushed to his breaking point after hearing what was to be Lincoln's last White House speech (in which Lincoln discussed the Emancipation Proclamation and teased a future announcement on the topic of African American citizenship), Booth determined to kill, rather than kidnap, the president, no matter what. In under seventy-two hours, Booth hatched a plan to draw on his connections at Ford's Theatre

and obtain access to the box where Lincoln, his wife, and commanding general Ulysses S. Grant were planning to see *Our American Cousin*. The assassin would take care of Lincoln and Grant, while his henchmen would eliminate Secretary of State William Seward and VP Andrew Johnson,

thereby setting the stage they hoped for the Confederates to reverse the trends of the time. Though the other three victims were not murdered, President Lincoln died at the hands of Booth, who cried, *"Sic semper tyrannis,"* or "Thus always to tyrants," into the crowd before disappearing into the night.

Tracked down by investigators at a farm in Virginia, the assassin supposedly declared, "Tell mother I die for my country," before the barn he was hiding in was set on fire. He was shot upon exiting the blazing structure.

➔ THE STORY OF HIS SEX LIFE

Though he never wed, Booth was rumored to be secretly engaged to Lucy Lambert Hale, the daughter of a U.S. Senator from New Hampshire. He was found with a snapshot of her in his pocket when he died. It would be romantic if the circumstances weren't so awful.

➔ WHY HE MATTERS

John Wilkes Booth set the template for political assassination in the modern age. There was plotting, intrigue, mystery, a solitary gunman, and a public venue. It also forced the government to evaluate how it would handle such tragedies in the future. Booth remains a profound symbol of the intense antipathy that subsisted between North and South at the time.

BEST FEATURES: **Nothing but his pretty face.**

"His figure is slender, but compact and well made. He has a small, finely formed head, with cold, classic features, a bright eye, and a face capable of great expression," wrote the *Philadelphia Press* in a review of one of his plays. Much like countless great and terrible orators of history, Booth had a charisma that carried him a little too far. He was easy on the eyes but a hard man to be around for too long.

HEAT FACTOR: **Colder than an assassin's blade.**

Don't judge a book by its cover and certainly don't judge Booth by his (unnervingly) attractive appearance. Booth had a nice moustache and a lot of swagger, but his profound racism, his delusions of grandeur, and his fondness for murder on a world-historical scale turn the scales against him. He was an insecure, unstable man who appeared to have some difficulty distinguishing between the actions on the stage and the reality of the world in front of him.

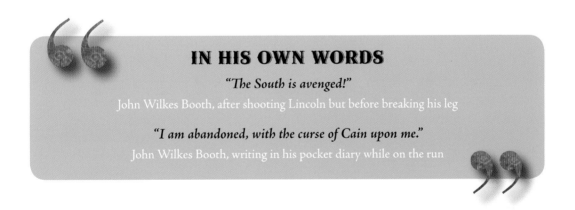

IN HIS OWN WORDS

"The South is avenged!"
John Wilkes Booth, after shooting Lincoln but before breaking his leg

"I am abandoned, with the curse of Cain upon me."
John Wilkes Booth, writing in his pocket diary while on the run

NIKOLA TESLA

"the man who invented the twentieth century"

VITAL STATS

YEARS: *1856 – 1943*

COUNTRY OF ORIGIN: *Croatia*

AREA OF INFLUENCE: *Science*

STYLE OF SEDUCTION:
Shockin' your body, meltin' your heart, and blowin' your mind

Nikola Tesla was a visionary scientist who had a real impact on the world we live in today. He also spoke eight languages, had a photographic memory, and was decades ahead of his time in a wide variety of scientific fields.

✦ TESLA'S LIFE STORY

Tesla was born in Croatia, which was then part of the Austro-Hungarian Empire. His father, an

Orthodox priest, wanted him to follow in his footsteps as a man of the cloth, but young Nikola instead took after his mother, who had a knack for mechanical invention. At just twenty-four, Tesla came up with the idea for the induction motor and was the driving force behind the development of alternating current (AC) power, a huge improvement on the way energy was conducted back then. Tesla's breakthrough really was a big one—we still use AC technology today to do everything from turning on the bathroom light to powering factories.

Tesla knew he needed a partner to help turn AC power from a set of drawings into a reality, and in 1884, he moved to America hoping to work for the inventor of the lightbulb, Thomas Edison. The two men collaborated for only a few months before things got messy. Trusting in the power of his own genius, Tesla quit, beginning an intellectual war with Edison, which played itself out over the course of a decade.

At the time, Edison was promoting direct current (DC) power transmission. It did the job of lighting lamps, but only low voltages could be sent out, and they couldn't make it more than a mile from one of Edison's power plants. Tesla's AC power sent much higher voltages, and it sent them much farther as well. Threatened, Edison and other DC supporters tried to characterize high-voltage AC as dangerous, even going so far as to arrange for a death row inmate to be electrocuted on a chair driven by AC power.

What became known as the "War of the Currents" ended after Westinghouse, the company Tesla worked for, got the contract to use its AC power at the 1893 World's Fair. If you want to show the public how powerful your technology is, there are few more powerful ways of doing that than by bringing light where once there was darkness at a global publicity event. Another Westinghouse contract enabled the company to harness the power of Niagara Falls in order to provide electricity throughout the United States.

When he wasn't engaged in practical questions about how to provide electricity cheaply and efficiently to the greatest number of people possible, Tesla was skipping from scientific discovery to scientific discovery with little regard for either his fortune or his legacy. He often neglected to file patents or even to write things down, but nonetheless, dozens of his inventions and discoveries are still in use today. From radio to radar to the VSTOL (vertical short takeoff and landing) plane, Tesla's influence is everywhere.

He was also a little bit crazy, as you might expect, and his lack of interest in worldly matters probably contributed to his sad end—alone and in debt, in a New York hotel room.

➢ THE STORY OF HIS SEX LIFE

There's not much of a story to tell, as Tesla remained celibate for his entire life. Preferring to focus any and all creative energy he had on his craft, he explained to one reporter that he had never married because married men were not great inventors. (Both his fear of women's pearls and his obsession with pigeons seem to make weird sense in conjunction with his disdain for human relationships.)

➢ WHY HE MATTERS

While Tesla didn't invent alternating current, he made it practical for use by us common folk—and that was an enormous boon to culture as a whole.

Powering our homes the way we do today would not be possible without his proofs in this field. He was also a prolific inventor, obtaining more than seven hundred patents in his lifetime. Some of his inventions that are still relevant today include the first wireless remote control boat, fluorescent and neon lights, and even vital functions in robotics.

Look Sirs, no hands!

DEATH BEAM

In 1934, page one of the *New York Times* read: "Tesla, at 78, Bares New Death Beam." Sensationalist headlines were common around this time, and a "Death Beam" wasn't *quite* what Tesla had in mind. His plan, laid out in a letter requesting financial support, was to save humanity by allotting each country one of the same weapon, so that each could feel protected without having to develop new implements of destruction. If everyone has the exact same capacity for destruction, then they'd all leave each other alone, and world peace would be ensured. The progress of the project ended there, though, due to lack of funding. The fact remains that Tesla thought he had a weapon that would be more powerful than anything else anyone could really imagine—and who are we to doubt him? Thank goodness he was one of the good guys.

✦ BEST FEATURE: **His integrity.**

Scientific integrity was so important to this guy that he lived an entirely sexless life so as to not get distracted from his scientific pursuits. Tesla went through life observing everything in the world around him, while remaining blind to anything—including relationships and entertainment—that could serve as a diversion. Often sporting a smug, do-you-know-who-I-am smirk, Tesla never backed down from a public fight if he believed he was in the right.

the smirk

✦ HEAT FACTOR: **He may have had good looks, but he also only had eyes for science.**

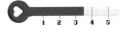

Nothing is more attractive than a big throbbing brain and a well-parted head of hair. Tesla fought and won a battle with one of America's most famous (and most diabolical) inventors and he harnessed the power of Niagra Falls. He also had a softer side—he came up with the idea for the induction motor while reciting poetry to a friend during a Budapest sunset. Sure, he died alone as a germophobic recluse, but that doesn't mean he wasn't worth loving. So long as you're cool with long-distance relationships, that is.

QUOTABLES

"*Were we to seize and eliminate from our industrial world the results of Mr. Tesla's work, the wheels of industry would cease to turn, our electric cars and trains would stop, our towns would be dark, our mills would be dead and idle. Yes, so far reaching is his work that it has become the warp and woof of industry.*"

B. A. Behrend

"*Tesla, you don't understand our American humor.*"

Thomas Edison, in response to Tesla's request for the $1 million promised him by the inventor

"*Nikola Tesla is the world's greatest inventor, not only at present but in all history. . . . His basic as well as revolutionary discoveries, for sheer audacity, have no equal in the annals of the intellectual world.*"

Hugo Gernsback

TEDDY ROOSEVELT

"the Colonel"

VITAL STATS

YEARS: *1858 – 1919*

COUNTRY OF ORIGIN: *USA*

AREA OF INFLUENCE: *Politics*

STYLE OF SEDUCTION:
*Ridin' rough and
dealin' square*

N⁰ 12

Teddy Roosevelt was the youngest president in American history, but it's hard to imagine he was surprised by his rapid rise to the top. Roosevelt was intelligent, talented, ambitious, and overwhelmingly positive in his outlook. He remains one of America's most well-regarded presidents.

ROOSEVELT'S LIFE STORY

Theodore "Teddy" Roosevelt was born into a wealthy New York City family in 1858 and raised in Manhattan. After high school, this go-getter went to Harvard and was elected to the New York State Assembly at the age of twenty-three.

(Twenty-three!) But tragedy struck at a young age, too, when both his wife and his mother died on the same day in 1884, sending him into a tailspin. To deal with (or possibly evade) his grief, Roosevelt moved to a ranch in what is now North Dakota. He threw himself into western life, driving cattle, hunting big game, and even receiving a post as a frontier sheriff. After two years of Wild West livin', he traveled to London, where he married his childhood sweetheart Edith Carrow.

Back in New York, Roosevelt resumed his political life and was appointed head of the U.S. Civil Service Commission, president of the New York City Board of Police Commissioners, and assistant secretary of the navy (after President McKinley appointed him to the position in 1897). When the Spanish-American War broke out in 1898, Roosevelt left the navy and, in a move worthy of a musical montage, rounded up his Wild West friends, formed a volunteer cavalry regiment (the "Rough Riders"), and led them to

victory in the Battle of San Juan Hill. When he returned to the United States, he was a hero.

Banking on his war-hero fame, the Republican Party backed Roosevelt in his successful run for governor of New York in 1898, and two years later they put him on the national presidential ticket as vice president to McKinley. McKinley won the election by a landslide, but Roosevelt served only six months as veep. On September 6, 1901, McKinley was shot and killed by an anarchist in Buffalo, making Roosevelt the youngest president in American history.

President Roosevelt became known as a trust-buster, fighting corporate interests and laying the groundwork for the Federal Trade Commission (FTC), which still regulates the industry today. He was also a dedicated conservationist, setting aside 200 million acres of land for national forests and wildlife refuges. After determining that the United States needed to play a bigger role on the world stage, he beefed up the navy, oversaw the treaty that gave the United States the right to build the Panama Canal, and negotiated the end of the Russo-Japanese War in 1905, a move that earned him the Nobel Peace Prize. So, yeah, he stayed busy.

After finishing his second term in office, Roosevelt left the presidency in the hands of fellow Republican William Howard Taft and went on a

safari in Africa. When he returned to America (with some five thousand animal skins in tow), Roosevelt realized that Taft had veered sharply to the right. Roosevelt challenged Taft for the Republican nomination in 1912, but when his party stuck with Taft, he created the Progressive (or Bull Moose) Party and ran on *its* ticket instead. While he was far more popular than Taft, he only succeeded in splitting the vote, and they were both trounced by Democratic nominee Woodrow Wilson. Even when his political career was over, Roosevelt continued to be a prolific writer, publishing dozens of books over his lifetime. He died in 1919 of a heart attack. And although he never seemed to so much as blink in the course of his lifetime, he died in his sleep. Even more ironically, he died peacefully.

THE BOOKER T. WASHINGTON SCANDAL

In 1901, Theodore Roosevelt invited Booker T. Washington (the former slave turned educator and political advisor) to dinner at the White House. This monumental gesture marked the first time an African American had attended a presidential meal. The country, of course, was still in a period of official racial segregation, and this supper signified that President Roosevelt considered Washington a social equal. America's reaction? Outrage, mainly in the form of political cartoons bearing vulgar depictions of the First Lady, insinuations that Washington never even made it to the dining table, and so on. It wasn't pretty, but it was progress.

➔ THE STORY OF HIS SEX LIFE

Not much to say here. He was married twice—first to Alice, who died at a young age, and then to Edith, his high school sweetheart. What a softie.

➔ WHY HE MATTERS

Roosevelt was the twenty-sixth president of the United States, a badass outdoorsman, a rancher, a hero of the Spanish-American War, the winner of a Nobel Peace Prize, and the country's first environmentalist. All his life he stuck to the things that interested *him*, first and foremost, but everywhere he went, he made a major impact and is still counted among the greatest of all American presidents.

→ **BEST FEATURE: His earnestness.**

Roosevelt was the perfect combination of rugged adventurer, egg-headed brainiac, and enthusiastic charmer. Teddy's bushy moustache, tiny frameless glasses, and sandy comb-over proclaim nothing if not gobs of character. Adaptable to every situation, Roosevelt navigated through everything from White House politics to an African safari, and strode his way right into America's hearts.

→ **HEAT FACTOR: Put it this way: The man even looks good in fringed leather and a fur cap.**

1 2 3 4 5

"No man has had a happier life than I have led; a happier life in every way." The sheer—seemingly unaffected—self-satisfaction of Teddy Roosevelt is reason enough to pencil his initials on your notebook. Sure, he wasn't perfect, and he certainly wasn't a friend to all (despite his love of nature, he wasn't afraid to kill animals), but then again, who is? In his prime, he was hard to beat, and even if history books may have dumped some of his more anachronistic tendencies, it's hard to say no to that steely gaze.

THE SPEECH SHOOTING INCIDENT

The Progressive Party's nickname, the Bull Moose Party, came from a failed assassination attempt on Roosevelt's life in Milwaukee, Wisconsin, in 1912. John Schrank shot a .32-caliber bullet at Roosevelt's heart, but the bullet was deterred by the case of the former president's signature glasses. Taking a moment to recover, Teddy then pulled the marred speech script out of his breast pocket and proclaimed, "It takes more than that to kill a Bull Moose."

IN HIS OWN WORDS

"Speak softly and carry a big stick; you will go far."

"Believe you can and you're halfway there."

ANNIE OAKLEY

VITAL STATS

YEARS: *1860 – 1926*

COUNTRY OF ORIGIN: *USA*

AREA OF INFLUENCE:
Marksmanship

STYLE OF SEDUCTION:
Shootin' straight

No. 13

> A born sharpshooter who could hit a hundred targets in a row from sixteen yards away, Annie Oakley rose up from her hardscrabble roots to become as famous as any male showman of the Wild West.

→ OAKLEY'S LIFE STORY

Born Phoebe Ann Moses to an impoverished, widowed mother with a large brood of children to support, the future Annie Oakley moved away from home before her tenth birthday. She was sent to the Darke County Infirmary, a group home for orphans, the elderly, and the mentally ill. At the age of ten, she was hired out to a nasty local family she referred to as "the wolves." She ran away as a young teenager, reuniting with her mother and her mother's new  husband. The old homestead wasn't any more prosperous than when she left, so Annie learned to shoot small game, which she sold to a local grocery store. She was such a good shot that she was able to pay her mother's mortgage with the profits from her kills.

Word of Annie's rifle skills spread far and wide. When she was fifteen, a Cincinnati hotel owner invited her to compete against a famous traveling marksman by the name of Frank E. Butler. Hitting twenty-five out of twenty-five targets to Butler's twenty-four, she won the match and his heart: The two were married the following year.

Annie's sharp-shooting skills lay dormant until 1882, when Frank's performance partner got sick, and Annie jumped at the chance to fill in. She stole the show, adopted the stage name of Annie Oakley, and joined the vaudeville circuit with her husband. Annie's sewing skills came in handy on the road; she made her own costumes and dressed like a real cowgirl. Annie quickly became the biggest act of Buffalo Bill Cody's Wild West Show. Crowds turned out in droves to see her shoot a dime tossed in the air from ninety feet away. Her friend, the Lakota chief and holy man Sitting Bull, gave her the nickname "Little Sure Shot." Her fame even  brought her to the court of Queen Victoria, who marveled at the "very clever little girl."

Oakley's career continued until shortly after her fortieth birthday, when she was seriously injured in a train accident. She took a leave of absence from sharpshooting, during which time she starred on the stage in a melodrama, *The Western Girl*. She returned to professional marksmanship, performing well into her fifties. When World War I started, she offered to recruit women and train soldiers as sharpshooters. The government refused her, so she raised money for the Red Cross by holding shooting demonstrations instead. The straight-shooting do-gooder set her last record at the age of sixty-two and passed away four years later.

✦ The Story of Her Sex Life

Annie Oakley remained married to Frank Butler from the age of sixteen until her death at sixty-six. The couple performed together, shot together, and saw the world together. After Annie died, Butler followed just eighteen days later.

✦ Why She Matters

Annie Oakley became a legendary figure in spite of her hardscrabble upbringing. She was a proto-feminist, a philanthropist, and a dedicated showman. Composer Irving Berlin even immortalized her in the Broadway smash, *Annie Get Your Gun*.

✦ Best Feature: **Her aim.**

Oakley was always graceful, even when shooting a dime at ninety feet. As a woman working in a man's world, she held her own and made a name for herself, while paving the way for future generations of women in the process.

the graceful sharpshooter

ANNIE GET YOUR GUN

Premiering on Broadway in May 1946, *Annie Get Your Gun* is perhaps the single most memorable tribute to the iconic markswoman. With music and lyrics by Irving Berlin, the musical centers on the romance between Oakley and her beau, Frank Butler. Their relationship is ridden with strife when Butler becomes overwhelmingly jealous of his GF's success and splits. In a wild twist, chief Sitting Bull ends up adopting the abandoned sharpshooter, but we'll stop there so as not to ruin the ending. The show was revived in 1966 and then again in 1999, with a film adaptation thrown into the mix in 1950. The über-successful, Tony-winning musical played to audiences of over a thousand and spawned the classic tune "There's No Business Like Show Business." The song has been covered dozens of times by the likes of Ethel Merman, Liza Minelli, and even lip-synchers on *RuPaul's Drag Race*.

→ HEAT FACTOR: **Who could resist a sharp-shooting philanthropist in a circle skirt?**

Annie Oakley wore her long hair loose, wore skirts over leggings to accentuate her athletic figure, and made her own clothes to perfectly fit her tiny frame. In the process of becoming a revolutionary female sharpshooter, she also became something of a trendsetter.

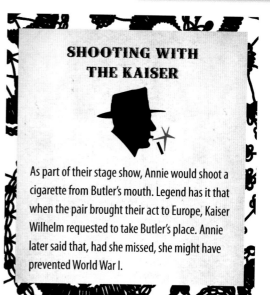

SHOOTING WITH THE KAISER

As part of their stage show, Annie would shoot a cigarette from Butler's mouth. Legend has it that when the pair brought their act to Europe, Kaiser Wilhelm requested to take Butler's place. Annie later said that, had she missed, she might have prevented World War I.

QUOTABLES

"The greatest woman rifle shot the world has ever produced."

Will Rogers

"I think that what she projected was a vitality and freshness that for many people came to stand for American womanhood. It's what made American women attractive: that outdoor complexion, that wonderful figure, and yet that carriage, that demureness, that suggested that she was in charge of herself and not to be had."

historian Paul Fees

"She's a very powerful woman and we are here today still honoring her because of all the examples she set. . . . She stood up for what she believed in. She traveled the world. She performed in front of queens, probably presidents, too . . . and she was very, very respected. So she's a lady I've always looked up to and was kind of always there in the back of my mind, kind of 'What would Annie do in a situation like this?'"

Reba McEntire, upon receiving the Annie Oakley Society Award

NELLIE BLY

"daredevil, feminist, reporter"

VITAL STATS

YEARS: *1864 – 1922*

COUNTRY OF ORIGIN: *USA*

AREA OF INFLUENCE:
Journalism

STYLE OF SEDUCTION:
Pushin' the envelope

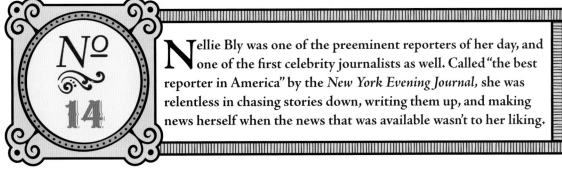

No.
14

Nellie Bly was one of the preeminent reporters of her day, and one of the first celebrity journalists as well. Called "the best reporter in America" by the *New York Evening Journal*, she was relentless in chasing stories down, writing them up, and making news herself when the news that was available wasn't to her liking.

→ BLY'S LIFE STORY

Nellie Bly (originally Elizabeth Jane Cochran) was born to a family of fifteen children in the Pennsylvanian small town of Cochran's Mills. The town had been named after Bly's father, a landowner and judge, and although the family was wealthy and influential at the outset, things fell apart when the patriarch died without leaving a will. Elizabeth enrolled in boarding school in the hopes of supporting her family as a teacher, but quickly dropped out due to lack of funds.

Desperate to support her kids and escape her abusive second ex-husband, Elizabeth's mother moved to Pittsburgh (a booming metropolis in comparison to Cochran's Mills) with her daughter in tow, with the idea that they'd have an easier time finding work there. That was no small task, however, for a woman in the nineteenth century, but the stars aligned when Elizabeth stumbled upon a column in the *Pittsburgh Dispatch* that left her incensed. The author found the presence of women in the workplace appalling and proposed they just stick to cooking and cleaning.

Having grown up with plenty of lady friends who had to work to keep their family businesses going, Bly penned a fiery, anonymous rebuttal so witty that, once the editor found out who she was, he hired her as a reporter at the rate of $5 per week and gave her the pen name Nellie Bly.

As a reporter, Bly grew frustrated with the female-centric beats she was given in fashion and the arts. So in order to rustle up a new story, Bly traveled to Mexico and spent six months sending dispatches about the Porfirio Díaz dictatorship. To her dismay, upon returning she was again assigned to fluff pieces. Sick and tired of being patronized, Bly went straight to the heart of America's hard-hitting news—New York City. After six months of job searching, she finally barked up the right tree at Joseph Pulitzer's office and snapped up a reporter position at the *New York World*.

At the *World*, Bly was free to report on the stories that interested her, and she blossomed into a star reporter. Riled by rumors of abuse at women's insane asylums, she posed as an unstable woman herself and reported the story from the inside. Her story on substan-

NELLIE PRACTICES INSANITY AT HOME.

dard conditions led to mental health care reform, and gave her quite a bit of street cred. What catapulted Nellie Bly from a "great reporter" into a full-fledged celebrity was her willingness to make herself the story. The famous thrill-seeker lived to be fifty-seven, when she died of a fatal grapple with pneumonia.

➔ THE STORY OF HER SEX LIFE

Money was a source of major anxiety for Nellie Bly growing up, so perhaps it's not surprising that when she had the chance to get more comfortable, she took it. She married industrialist Robert Seaman when she was thirty and he was seventy. It was a classic case of beauty and the bazillionaire, because, factoring in inflation, the manufacturing CEO's salary was officially ginormous. Bly inherited the fortune upon his death a decade later, but as they say, "mo' money, mo' problems," and after seeing her bank account dwindle due to a variety of embezzlement problems, she wound up bankrupt. Perhaps simply too independent to ever really settle down, Bly then returned to her first love, journalism and remained single for the rest of her life.

➔ WHY SHE MATTERS

Nellie Bly paved the way for female journalists, demonstrating that women's reporting didn't have to be restricted to fashion shows and social events. Beyond this, Bly initiated a new brand of reporting: stunt journalism—the one-year blog project of its time. Her blunt writing and her fearlessness are immortalized by an amusement park in Brooklyn that once bore her name but which is now simply called "Adventurer's."

INSPIRATION FOR HER GLOBE-TROTTING

If her showstopping feats weren't enough to make us flip, Bly really sealed the deal with her appreciation for a good sci-fi novel. Her admiration for Jules Verne, author of *20,000 Leagues Under the Sea*, was so strong that she felt compelled to follow in the footsteps of one of his protagonists, Phileas Fogg, who circumnavigated the globe in eighty days in Verne's novel, appropriately titled *Around the World in 80 Days*. She charted the same course as the fictional voyager, stopping for a meet-and-greet with the author himself in Europe, and packed nearly the same contents as he did in her parcels. Fogg did manage to one-up her slightly, winning £20,000 in a bet as a result, but Bly managed to set the record as the first real, live human to complete the daunting task.

❖ BEST FEATURE: **Her bravery.**

From moving from the country to the city, to traveling around the world, there was no challenge that Bly would shy away from and little that she wouldn't do in pursuit of a story. She's the archetype of the hard-hitting, bullheaded reporter. There was hardly any delay in her progression from "Hey, I've got an idea . . . " to "See ya later, boss—I'm gonna see if I can make some contacts in the black market baby-selling trade!" The "pretty crazy girl" with the sensible hairstyle would not be stopped—nothing got between her and a story.

❖ HEAT FACTOR: **Hot off the presses— literally!**

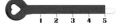

From her full-length houndstooth jacket, to her no-frills black leather satchel, to her aggressive style of journalism, Nellie Bly was the complete package. Each time fate tossed her a curveball, she shaped a new destiny for herself. And you've gotta love a low-maintenance girl; on her months-long trip around the world, Bly brought only one dress, a nighty, a blazer, and a few changes of underwear. Oh, and she brought a flask, too.

no-frills satchel
(flask within)

IN HER OWN WORDS

"Never having failed, I could not picture what failure meant."
"From Jersey Back to Jersey," *New York World*

"Energy rightly applied and directed will accomplish anything."

"It is only after one is in trouble that one realizes how little sympathy and kindness there are in the world."

"Accept praise for its worth—politeness. Be brutally frank with yourself. It's safer."

"If one would become great, two things are absolutely necessary. The first is to know yourself. The second is not to let the world know you."

W.E.B. DUBOIS

"The cost of liberty is less than the price of repression."

VITAL STATS

YEARS: 1868 – 1963

COUNTRY OF ORIGIN: USA

AREAS OF INFLUENCE: Sociology, Civil Rights

STYLE OF SEDUCTION: Breakin' down the barriers between us, baby

Nº 15

A author and sociologist William Edward Burghardt DuBois dedicated his life to fighting the oppression of African Americans, post–World War II. The most famous expression of his beliefs was his book *The Souls of Black Folk.*

→ DuBois's Life Story

W.E.B. DuBois was born in Massachusetts in 1868, during Andrew Jackson's presidency and not long after the conclusion of the Civil War. With ancestors who had fought in the Revolutionary War and parents of relatively high social standing, DuBois's family was not a victim of the still fresh wounds of slavery in the way many of his peers were (but that's not to say they did not suffer their own significant share of abuse and prejudice). After graduating as high school valedictorian, DuBois headed south to Nashville's Fisk University to study liberal arts while teaching black students in neighboring schools. Aiming straight for the top, he enrolled in a PhD program at Harvard and commenced work on a long and

winding history of the slave trade. Upon completion of the history in 1895, he turned heads as the first African American to graduate from the top-ranked Ivy League university.

Having spent his grad school years as one of the first students to approach sociology from a scientific perspective (so as to eliminate bias due to race or other subjective factors), DuBois found it pretty tricky to make progress working on race relations at the University of Atlanta. After publishing *The Philadelphia Negro: A Social Study 1899*, the first case study of the black community, DuBois became aggravated with academic pursuits that just weren't making a difference and instead found a new focus in direct, straightforward protest.

In 1903, his now classic book *The Souls of Black Folk* debuted, presenting in layman's terms the same case he'd been making for decades. Arguing against a tolerant, peaceful, and *gradual* solution to persistent racism, he was classified as a "radical" activist in his day. Capitalizing on his newfound soapbox, DuBois founded the Niagara Movement two years later to combat the social hierarchy of the time, then later helped lay the groundwork for the National Association for

DuBois

Advancement of Colored People, which is still in existence today. Through his work speaking on behalf of the NAACP, DuBois brought global attention to the maltreatment of former slaves and of blacks in general in the United States by pointing out the way American racism mimicked the dynamics of subjugated peoples internationally, as a result of colonization.

He moved further and further away from the American mainstream (both white and black) as he aged, becoming a Communist calling for an elimination of atomic weapons at a time when Americans felt particularly vulnerable, and even advocating voluntary segregation. Nevertheless, upon his death in 1963, he was honored with a state funeral and possessed dozens of honorary degrees and awards in recognition of his work.

✦ THE STORY OF HIS SEX LIFE

DuBois's family life was way less controversial than his public life, and he spent more than half a century married to his first wife, Nina Gomer, with whom he raised two kids. A year after her death in 1950, he married fellow activist and author Shirley Graham, who stayed by his side until his death twelve years later.

W.E.B. DUBOIS VS. BOOKER T. WASHINGTON

Although much of his commentary may sound like common sense today, the fact is that DuBois was seen as a radical in his time, and conservative civil rights mover-and-shaker Booker T. Washington had more than a little to do with shaping that rep. A Republican who preached self-help and insisted that America become color blind, Washington held super-conservative ideals that flew in the face of DuBois's urgent call to action. The public dispute forced the black community to pick sides, resulting in two rigid schools of thought within the civil rights movement—and little peace for either man. But sometimes that's the price of progress.

✦ WHY HE MATTERS

Growing up amid a frenzy of change after the Civil War emancipated slaves in America, DuBois saw that something still had to be done about the status quo. It would take a lot more than waiting for things to change in order for African Americans to actually gain equality. First on paper and later through megaphone, DuBois made no bones about his disregard for those—black *and* white—who believed the social pecking order was something enduring, something that couldn't be budged. After years of scholarly research didn't have the effect he desired, DuBois didn't back down; he leapt up, took to the podium, and made sure the public heard his voice in decrying the state blacks were living in even after they'd gained their legal freedoms. Once he had everyone's attention, he put organizations like the NAACP into place to help preserve the rights that he was fighting to win.

⇢ BEST FEATURE: **His honesty.**

In almost every line quoted today from the works of DuBois, you can hear his yearning for truth and for a reckoning with that truth—however hard it may have been to confront. In every study he put together and every book he wrote, his message boiled down to seeking the truth, then spreading the message to everyone he could. DuBois was and remains the poster boy for real talk.

⇢ HEAT FACTOR: **Positively burning (with the desire for change).**

With a thick beard and fluffy moustache framing his pillowy lips, and a razor-sharp mind, W.E.B. DuBois was a helluva figure to strike up a conversation with. He was most likely compatible with someone who could keep up with his debate tactics. We only docked him a point for his über-extremist views that translated into a lack of tolerance as he aged. Otherwise, we're bestowing our blessing on anyone who can get a word in edgewise.

IN HIS OWN WORDS

"Herein lies the tragedy of the age: not that men are poor—all men know something of poverty; not that men are wicked—who is good? Not that men are ignorant—what is Truth? Nay, but that men know so little of men."

"The main thing is the YOU beneath the clothes and skin—the ability to do, the will to conquer, the determination to understand and know this great, wonderful, curious world."

"I do not laugh. I am quite straight-faced as I ask soberly: 'But what on earth is whiteness that one should so desire it?' Then always, somehow, some way, silently but clearly, I am given to understand that whiteness is the ownership of the earth forever and ever, Amen!"

"There is always a certain glamour about the idea of a nation rising up to crush an evil simply because it is wrong. Unfortunately, this can seldom be realized in real life; for the very existence of the evil usually argues a moral weakness in the very place where extraordinary moral strength is called for."

CZARINA ALEXANDRA

"the last empress of Russia"

№ 16

Alexandra was a strong-willed and superstitious woman—a particularly bad combination of character traits in a ruler. With a little help from her friend Rasputin (and the Russian people, too), Alexandra Feodorovna Romanova brought down the Russian monarchy, paving the way for the Communist revolution.

ROMANOVA'S LIFE STORY

The future czarina was born Princess Alix Victoria Helena Louise Beatrice of Hesse and by Rhine, daughter of the German Grand Duke of Hesse-Darmstadt and the granddaughter of Queen Victoria of England. Princess Alix's childhood was troubled; her mother died when she was six years old, and both her brother and one of her sisters died at young ages. When she was twelve, her family traveled to St. Petersburg to attend a wedding, and it was then that she met her future husband, Nicholas II. The two married nearly a decade later, and she assumed a new name, Alexandra Feodorovna Romanova, a moniker befitting her station as the soon-to-be empress of Russia.

Shy and reserved, Alexandra wasn't too popular in the Russian court. Her popularity with the people of Russia waned, too, when she wholeheartedly embraced both Russian Orthodoxy and the idea that her husband should be an absolute ruler over the country. She believed it was her sacred duty to make sure that Nicholas's limited power became total.

During the early years of their marriage, Alexandra bore five children. Tragedy struck the royal family when Alexandra's son, Alexei, next in line to become the czar, fell ill with hemophilia, a genetic disorder that keeps the blood from clotting. After doctors' attempts to heal her son failed, the superstitious Alexandra enlisted the help of a monk and mystic healer named Grigory Rasputin to stop her son's frequent hemorrhages. Rasputin promised her that Alexei wouldn't die and prayed for him. In a seemingly miraculous turn of events, Alexei started to get better. Though at first the Russian people venerated Rasputin as a holy man, he soon fell from grace and was distrusted by the country at large. But no matter what her people thought, Alexandra trusted Rasputin completely. She was a self-proclaimed worrier, and Rasputin's decisive nature likely put her at ease about many of her weighty royal decisions. When World War I began and Emperor Nicholas

Rasputin: mystic monk or psychic sorcerer?

went off to the Eastern Front, Alexandra gave Rasputin even more power, silencing his critics and allowing him to replace members of the royal cabinet with his cronies.

The Russian people were aghast at Alexandra's antics, as were fellow political leaders and nobles, many of which convened and decided to kill Rasputin in an effort to save the reputation of the Russian monarchy. This proved a difficult task: First they poisoned Rasputin. Then, when the poison didn't seem to take effect, they shot him. Rasputin fell to the ground, but rose again moments later and tried to escape. They shot him again, tied him up, and threw him in a frozen river.

Even after Rasputin's murder, the damage Alexandra had done to the image of the Russian monarchy proved irreversible. When the Russian Revolution began in February of 1917, Nicholas abdicated his right to the throne. The abdication was not enough for the revolutionaries, however, for in July of 1918, Alexandra, Nicholas, and their children were executed.

➤ THE STORY OF HER SEX LIFE

By all accounts, the union between Alexandra and Nicholas was a true love match, one that began while both were still children. Marrying for love was rare for royals in those days, and Alexandra and Nicholas were a lucky pair. The couple had five children together, four girls and, finally, a boy.

➤ WHY SHE MATTERS

Alexandra was superstitious, listened to the wrong people, and ignored her advisors when they confronted her with their misgivings. All in all, she was not a person you would want running your country. Her poor decisions, along with a lot of other political factors, led to the permanent downfall of the Russian monarchy.

**the last czarina
and czar of Russia**

THE ROYAL DISEASE

Hemophilia was once known as "the royal disease." The genetic disorder, marked by the body's inability to form blood clots, can be traced back to Alexandra Romanova's grandmother, Queen Victoria of England. Victoria was aware of the genetic disorder and worried about its effects, once writing in a letter to her daughter: "I can't help thinking what dear Papa said—that it was in fact when there was some little imperfection in the pure Royal descent that some fresh blood was infused. . . . For that constant fair hair and blue eyes makes the blood so lymphatic . . . it is not as trivial as you may think, for darling Papa—often with vehemence said: 'We must have some strong blood.'" She may not have been a licensed medical practitioner, but her concerns were well founded. Hemophilia can now be treated with blood transfusions.

→ BEST FEATURE: **Her conviction.**

Even as the system crumbled around her, and even as her people became murderously enraged, Alexandra maintained her religious convictions, as well as a belief in her husband's sacred right as an absolute ruler. While she ended up on the wrong side of history, there's something to be said for sticking to your guns, even when everyone else is against you.

→ HEAT FACTOR: **She may have looked good in a tiara, but otherwise it's hard to find much to love about Alexandra Feodorovna Romanova.**

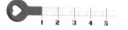

Alexandra's religious fanaticism, gullibility, and belief in the absolute power of kings are total turnoffs. She was a beautiful woman with a pale complexion, delicate features, and dark hair, but it's nearly impossible to find a picture of her with a smile.

unsmiling as ever

QUOTABLES

"Though it could hardly be said that the Czar governed Russia in a working sense, he ruled as an autocrat and was in turn ruled by his strong-willed if weak-witted wife. Beautiful, hysterical, and morbidly suspicious, she hated everyone but her immediate family and a series of fanatic or lunatic charlatans who offered comfort to her desperate soul."

historian Barbara W. Tuchman

". . . devoid of charm, wooden, cold eyes, holds herself as if she'd swallowed a yardstick."

Russian court's early description of Alexandra

HARRY HOUDINI

"Genius of Escape"

VITAL STATS

YEARS: *1874 – 1926*

COUNTRY OF ORIGIN: *Hungary*

AREA OF INFLUENCE:
Entertainment

STYLE OF SEDUCTION:
Breakin' (out of) your heart

N?
17

For magician Harry Houdini, no act was too outrageous. He made his name by popularizing escape acts that were pretty much nuts, from getting buried alive to being submerged underwater while wrapped in a straitjacket.

✦ HOUDINI'S LIFE STORY

Born to a Zionist rabbi and homemaking mother in Budapest in 1874, the young Houdini (born Ehrich Weiss) began tossing newspapers on neighbors' front porches and shining shoes to help support the family once they moved to the United States. After leaving home at the age of twelve to see the country on his own, the tween sent a letter home to his mother that was signed "Your truant son." He clearly had a sense of humor to go with his death wish. After Houdini returned, the family gave him a taste of adventure when they moved to New York City just a year later. The thirteen-year-old found a gig cutting fabric in a garment district factory. While experiencing success in sports in school (which would prove to be a great blessing in his later career), the future illusionist stumbled upon *Memoirs of Robert-Houdin: Ambassador, Author, Conjuror* and was immediately taken with the world of magic.

Adding a final *i* to Robert-Houdin's name to complement his budding onstage persona, Houdini began to teach himself tricks, booking himself at traveling fairs and amusement parks as

a part of the attractions. One of his first tricks was inspired simply by the materials around him: Houdini would ask witnesses to tie him up with nearby rope and lock him in a cabinet, and somehow he always managed to reemerge free of his restraints. This fascination with self-imposed bondage became a theme in his work, and calling himself the "Handcuff King," he used the shackles as a kind of trademark feature in his acts.

Houdini slowly gained notoriety in America as part of a double act with a menagerie of props

meant to utterly constrain his movements—locks and keys, straitjackets, sealed chests, and even coffins. But he grew impatient with his level of fame in the United States and took off on a European tour to amaze what he thought might be more easily impressed audiences across the Atlantic.

It did the trick, and he happily sailed to stardom while honing such acts as the Milk Can Escape, in which he folded himself into what was essentially a large metal milk bottle (large for a milk bottle, that is, not large for a human) that was then filled with water and sealed. After two minutes, out he would pop, having apparently held his breath and managed to force his way free despite a very limited sphere of movement. (It was later explained that the "seal" on the milk can was compromised, even though audiences couldn't detect it. Still, it was quite a trick.) A natural performer, he

began applying his unbelievable control over his body as a silent film actor and spent much of his final years adding to his written work on magic, which is now in the possession of the Library of Congress.

In October of 1926, at age fifty-two, Houdini accepted the challenge from a young man to deliver a few blows to his stomach. He had accepted these kinds of challenges numerous times before, but this time he was taken by surprise. After receiving the punches, he fell ill, his appendix ruptured, and he died of peritonitis on Halloween.

✦ THE STORY OF HIS SEX LIFE

Houdini met fellow performer Beatrice "Bess" Rahner—a Brooklyn girl born and raised—on the road and married her in 1894. They began touring as a double act with "The Beautiful Bess" as Harry's magician's assistant. The two lovers had agreed that should anything happen to Houdini during an act, she would attempt to make contact with him in the afterlife by means of a séance.

After making such attempts for a decade, the disenchanted Bess decided, "Ten years is long enough to wait for any man."

HOUDINI AND SPIRITUALISM

Even though Houdini and his wife agreed to try and stay in touch after he passed away, Houdini was deeply opposed to such activities and fought against them for much of his life. Houdini's acts relied in equal measure on planning, physical ability, and a few shortcuts, but it seems possible that his experience in showmanship contributed to his skepticism about "spiritualism"— the belief that souls survive after death and can be contacted via mediums, for instance. Spiritualism was very popular at the time. In fact, Sherlock Holmes creator Arthur Conan Doyle was himself a believer, and, since he and Houdini were friends, they engaged in a spirited debate on the topic for quite some time. (It remains unclear who exactly won that argument.) Like Doyle, Houdini appeared to want to believe but could never quite get there.

✦ WHY HE MATTERS

Houdini was entirely self-taught and driven by a passion for dazzling audiences with impossible feats. His legacy includes the invention of the escape from a straitjacket and the underwater chamber trick. Also high-lighting his résumé was the biggest feat attempted on a magician's stage: the disap-pearance of a live elephant. In an era of cabarets and flappers, Houdini took stage performance to a whole new level, setting a precedent for entertainers to push their acts to the limit.

⇢ BEST FEATURE: **His audacity.**

Preoccupied since childhood with what others told him was beyond the realm of possibility, Houdini made a name for himself by always push-ing the envelope. While his utter fearlessness in

pleasing crowds and pushing his own physical limits eventually may have contributed to his death, we're pretty sure he wouldn't have had it any other way.

⇢ HEAT RATING: **If you want to be a star, then you have to bring the heat.**

Houdini was obsessed with death. He was also obsessed with fame. He was short, stocky, and bowlegged. His pointy nose and reverse wid-ow's peak don't exactly say "come hither," but there's no denying the appeal of such a devoted risk-taker. There was pretty much nothing he wouldn't do. He was, without a doubt, a star.

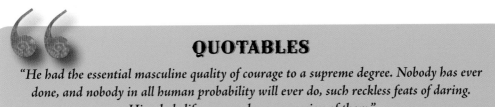

QUOTABLES

"He had the essential masculine quality of courage to a supreme degree. Nobody has ever done, and nobody in all human probability will ever do, such reckless feats of daring. His whole life was one long succession of them."

Sir Arthur Conan Doyle

"Houdini, the magician who debunked magic, could not bear to see the great rationalist [Arthur Conan] Doyle enchanted by ghosts and frauds. And so he did what any friend would: He set out to prove spiritualism false and rob his friend Doyle of the only comforting fiction that was keeping him sane. It was the least he could do."

comedian John Hodgman

"People either didn't believe Houdini when he said that his tricks on film were real, or they didn't care."

New York Times critic John Leonard

MATA HARI

"I am a woman who enjoys herself very much."

VITAL STATS

YEARS: *1876 – 1917*

COUNTRY OF ORIGIN: *Holland*

AREAS OF INFLUENCE:
Entertainment, Espionage

STYLE OF SEDUCTION:
Playin' you false

Nº 18

Margaretha Geertruida Zelle (aka "Lady MacLeod," aka "Mata Hari") was a Dutch exotic dancer who parlayed her liaisons with some of Europe's most prominent gentleman into a brief career in espionage. She played a high-stakes game with dangerous opponents during World War I, and it ended . . . badly.

☞ MATA HARI'S LIFE STORY

Margaretha Geertruida Zelle was born in a small Dutch town in 1876. Her father managed to achieve some financial success with his hat shop during Margaretha's youth, but when his wife died and his hat-making business faltered, Margaretha was sent to college to become a kindergarten teacher. An affair with her headmaster cut short her training, and with nothing to lose, she answered an ad in the newspaper from a colonial officer seeking a wife. She moved to the Dutch East Indies to be with him, but colonial life was horrible and her marriage worse, so she fled both to start a new life in Paris. (Starting new lives was never a problem for her.)

no mate for Mata

Margaretha thought that with her big dark eyes and long dark hair she would be a shoo-in for modeling work, but that didn't turn out to be the case. Nevertheless, instead of returning to Holland, she reinvented herself as Mata Hari, an exotic dancer of mysterious, vaguely Eastern origins. She debuted on the stage of Paris's Musée Guimet wearing an Indian sarong, jewelry from the museum's East Asian collection, and metal plates covering her chest. Her performance consisted of stripping and twirling seductively before the statue of the Hindu god of destruction. Audiences loved it, and soon she was the toast of Paris. She toured Europe, collecting gifts from smitten admirers in every city on the Continent.

At the peak of her fame, when she was pivoting from high-profile love affair to high-profile love affair, she became involved in international espionage, but the details remain muddy. Whatever her actions, the French government arrested her in 1917, locked her up for six months and then put her in front of a firing squad. Both the French and German governments would exculpate her years after her death.

The Story of Her Sex Life

Margaretha Geertruida Zelle's marriage to Rudolf MacLeod was even worse than what you'd expect from a teenager and a career colonialist who met through the newspaper. By all accounts, it was a total nightmare: MacLeod was a gambler, an alcoholic, had syphilis, and he was jealous and abusive. He was, in other words, just about the worst husband imaginable. Their deeply troubled marriage—along with their dangerously adventurous sex lives—had tragic implications for their children, one of whom died at the age of two. Some have speculated that the child's death was due to mercury poisoning, since at the time mercury was administered as treatment for syphilis (which, unfortunately, can be passed on to children).

After she adopted her new exotic persona, Mata Hari had lovers in abundance, and many of these happened to be military officers. During World War I, allegiances were tentative and enemies were everywhere, and the border-hopping dancer was, as a result, playing with fire. Her sex life was her professional life and vice versa, and when the end came, it was due more to love than it was to money. In order to obtain a pass across hostile borders to see her then lover—a Russian general named Vadime—she agreed to help provide information to the head of French intelligence. What she couldn't have known, however, was that the head of French intelligence suspected her of spying in France and wanted a big-name capture to show that France was making inroads against domestic espionage.

Why She Matters

Beautiful, mysterious, and seductive in the extreme, Mata Hari helped create the archetype of the femme fatale. In retrospect, it appears unlikely that she had any real impact on war campaigns or initiatives, but her exotic appearance and voracious sexual appetite were enough to instill fear and loathing in many Europeans. Wherever she went, she made an impression.

Best Feature: **Her ability to reinvent herself.**

Mata Hari, who came from nothing and transformed herself into the most desirable woman in the world, was the mother of reinvention. She was a self-made woman who used her looks and her wiles to make her own way in the world. And when her act started to slow down, she simply came up with something else. For a while there was simply no stopping her, because she was impossible to pin down. Her name, her appearance, her lover—nothing was static.

⇢ HEAT FACTOR: **Hot enough to play with fire, but not hot enough to do it for very long.**

1 2 3 4 5

The image of Mata Hari—gauzy scarves trailing down her bare back, a bold metallic chest piece, and an unapologetic expression on her face as she stares directly into the camera—still has the power to seduce. But the notion of trading on exotic stereotypes of other cultures has lost its luster over time. Mata Hari was ahead of her time in terms of how she lived her life, but in other ways, she really was a product (and a victim) of her time.

Though Mata Hari made quite a bit of noise during her life, the first time she was represented on-screen, it was actually in a silent film, in 1921. Subsequent attempts to commit her legendary tale to the screen often resulted in wildly speculative scripts, but their artful visuals and star power committed the myth to public memory. Celebrities like Greta Garbo, Marlene Dietrich, and Doris Day all flexed their actorly muscles to weave a tale of fact and fiction for American audiences. That being said, 1967's *Casino Royale* probably has the distinction of being more liberal with the truth: In that film, the character of Mata Hari appeared as the mother of James Bond's child. The baby girl, of course, bears the dancer's namesake. The legacy, like the mystery, continues . . .

QUOTABLES

"She was an over-rated young woman. Not a beauty—but she had charm. Yes. She had charm, and that's what counts. But beauty? No."

Andre Mornet, prosecutor of Mata Hari

"The problem was not what Mata Hari said but who she was. She was a woman travelling alone, obviously wealthy and an excellent linguist—too educated, too foreign. Worse yet, she admitted to having a lover. Women like that were immoral and not to be trusted."

biographer Pat Shipman

"I was not content at home. . . . I wanted to live like a colorful butterfly in the sun."

Mata Hari

ISADORA DUNCAN

"the mother of
modern dance"

VITAL STATS

YEARS: *1877 – 1927*

COUNTRY OF ORIGIN: *USA*

AREA OF INFLUENCE: *Dance*

STYLE OF SEDUCTION:
Movin' freely

No.
19

Isadora Duncan was perhaps the most famous dancer of her day. She was a major proponent of what we now identify as "modern dance," and her art drew heavily from her roller coaster of a life.

✦ DUNCAN'S LIFE STORY

Dora Angela Duncan was the youngest of four children born into a fairly unconventional household in San Francisco in 1877. The family was supported by Dora's father, Joseph Duncan (a bank-owning, art-selling, newspaper-running dynamo) and was presided over by Dora's mother, who was thirty years younger than her husband. Although he was ambitious in his business pursuits, Joseph didn't take well to hard times and abandoned the city and his family when his banking business collapsed. As a result, everyone in the newly impoverished family of five had to pitch in, and Little Miss Duncan accepted her first paying gig as a dancer at age six. She and her sister continued at school for a while (also learning ballet, burlesque, and the Delsarte technique), but then dropped out in order to teach dance as a means of supporting the rest of the family.

As an adult, Duncan lived a life that was as improvised, natural, and free as her dancing style. She bounced from Chicago to New York to London, where she finally settled for a bit in 1899. While there, she began to break free of the tropes and traditions of the day, dancing to music by Chopin and Beethoven instead of more traditional "dance music." Still bored, Duncan opened her own school in Germany in 1904, where she worked to overcome the "deforming" practices of ballet with her new, more natural style of dance. This dance troupe was soon branded "The Isadorables."

While many revolutionary artists do not enjoy fame during their lifetimes, Isadora Duncan enraged critics and thrilled audiences in equal measure, and was able to see her own image sculpted into the façade of the famous Théâtre des Champs-Élysées in Paris in 1913. Always on her feet but never tiring, Duncan went on to found two more dance schools—one in Paris and one in Moscow—all the while embarking on international tours with her unconstrained choreography.

Duncan was killed in France in 1927, when her scarf became tangled in the wheel of a sports car she was riding in, snapping her neck. It was the final chapter of her dramatic life.

⇨ The Story of Her Sex Life

Sure, proto-feminist Isadora Duncan didn't believe in marriage, but that didn't stop her from having a fling or twelve. The first, or perhaps just the first that received public attention, was with stage designer Edward Gordon Craig, who affectionately called Isadora "Topsy" throughout the four years of their relationship. She bore him a daughter, Deirdre. Her second *People* magazine–worthy affair was far more lucrative. With sewing machine heir Paris Singer, she

had her son Patrick, and Mr. Moneybags funded her second school for dance in France. Tragically, the two children died in a crash as bizarre as her own when their

car rolled into the Seine. During her stint in the Soviet Union, Duncan was married to the much younger poet Sergei Yesenin for a bit, despite the fact that neither one had a very solid grasp on the other's language. That didn't keep them from communicating, however, on the most important art questions of the day—and on more personal matters as well, one would assume.

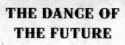

THE DANCE OF THE FUTURE

In 1903, Isadora Duncan delivered a speech in Berlin called "The Dance of the Future." Her treatise contrasted, in an almost academic fashion, ballet and a new, more natural form of dance—the type of movement that she believed is innate in rhythm and thus at the root of dance. After alluding to the minimalism of the classical Greeks, she described how ballet, with its rigorous choreography, physically destroys the body over time. Duncan emphasized that children should not be taught by imitation but instead should create their own movements. And so, slowly but surely, an age of dance as instinct was ushered in.

⇨ Why She Matters

Primarily influenced by the philosophies of the ancient Greeks and by Friedrich Nietzsche, Isadora founded what later came to be called simply "free dance." Women of the Victorian era had almost no power, either politically or socially. In breaking with tradition, Duncan was able to simultaneously liberate dance from its conception as a banal entertainment and liberate women—to a point—from their shackles as sexless figures fit only for domesticity.

✦ BEST FEATURE: **Her liberated nature.**

A 2003 dance piece performed by the Isadora Duncan Dance Foundation in New York was titled "Isadora . . . no apologies"—a phrase that could be used to describe her life as a whole. The glassy-eyed Duncan always kept her eyes firmly on the prize of elevating dance as a medium and liberating it as a means of expression. Even her flowy Grecian costumes drew attention to the body's movements rather than its form.

Isadora the Greek

✦ HEAT FACTOR: **In a (new) word, she was utterly (Is)adorable.**

Isadora's love life was almost as modern as her dance. She knew what she wanted and pursued it—whatever "it" might be. She proudly engaged in what others would have considered "compromising" correspondence, and she took pride in her physicality, both on stage and off. Oh, and she also wrote books, theorized about the future of dance, and paved the way for women's liberation in the twentieth century. She was hot because she thought she was. She had swagger.

QUOTABLES

"Isadora Duncan seems to me as innocent as a child dancing through the garden in the morning sunshine and picking the beautiful flowers of her fantasy."

Theodore Roosevelt

"Whatever Isadora did was Art."

John Dos Passos

"She employs no illusions, no cunningly arranged mirrors . . ., no beautifully multicolored lime-lights. Never was there anything less sensational than her work; it is severe in its simplicity. . . ."

St. Louis Sunday Gazette

"When we dance Isadora, we dance with the whole world. Our planet needs that."

Alice Bloch, in *Dance* magazine

MUSTAFA KEMAL ATATÜRK

"father of all Turks"

VITAL STATS

YEARS: *1881 – 1938*

COUNTRY OF ORIGIN:
What was once the Ottoman Empire, now Greece

AREA OF INFLUENCE: *Politics*

STYLE OF SEDUCTION:
Pushin' the pedal to the metal

No 20

Atatürk made headlines—and plenty of enemies—by helping form the country we know today as Turkey. After becoming Turkey's first president, he implemented sweeping reforms that modernized the culture of the entire country.

→ ATATÜRK'S LIFE STORY

Atatürk grew up to be a steadfast fighter, and his difficult beginnings probably contributed to his strong resolve. When Atatürk was a young boy, his father, a timber merchant, died suddenly, leaving Atatürk's uncle to care for the family. At the age of twelve, he decided to go to military school against his uncle's wishes. The young Atatürk proved a gifted student and a young activist, joining an underground group dedicated to overthrowing the Turkish dictator Abdullamid.

Upon his graduation in 1905, Atatürk became a captain in the military. Over the next ten years, he quickly ascended the chain of command, including leading a battle in Tripoli against the Italian forces. When the Ottoman Empire joined World War I,

CAPTAIN

Atatürk led several winning battles against the Allied forces and was promoted to colonel. His, um, enthusiasm for battle—and his stark prioritization of the group over the individual—is best illustrated by his famous, and startlingly blunt, command: "I don't order you to fight. I order you to die."

After World War I, Atatürk used his military prowess to fight for Turkish independence from the Ottoman Empire. He battled the sultan's army as well as Armenian and Greek armies, saving the new nation from a foreign invasion while clearing a path for a new Turkish state. In 1923, Turkey was recognized as a sovereign nation with Atatürk at the helm.

Before Atatürk, the Turkish people had lived in a Muslim theocracy. At the start of his reign, Atatürk set out to change all that. He abolished the sultan's Islamic political institutions, granted women political independence, and even changed the way people dressed. In short, he westernized Turkey right down to the alphabet, changing it from an Arabic base to a Latin one, a revolutionary move that renounced the old Ottoman Empire.

Atatürk was rewarded for his efforts with a lifelong reign and a heroic moniker: In 1935, the Turkish people adopted the Western habit of using last names. His means "Father of All Turks." Atatürk died of liver cancer at the age of fifty-seven.

TURKEY'S ACADEMIC ADVANCEMENT

One of Atatürk's biggest and unlikeliest fans was not another political leader but an important scientist from the United States—Albert Einstein. Despite his opinion that Atatürk was the most important leader of the twentieth century, Einstein turned down a personal invitation to come teach at one of Turkey's universities. Instead, he chose Princeton, stating coyly, "as fate would have it, it was not to be." In a letter to the Turkish leader dated September 17, 1933, Einstein implored Atatürk to allow Jewish medical students (who had been fired from their jobs as a result of Adolf Hitler's new anti-Semitic policies) to come study at his institutions instead. The political giant agreed to the mutually beneficial plan, which helped Atatürk, in turn, to further education reform and produce a more liberal and diverse system. These first forty students that Einstein bargained for opened the floodgates into Turkey's up-and-coming academic community, and over the next decade, hundreds more Western-educated students, professors, and professionals flocked to Istanbul in particular to learn and teach.

→ THE STORY OF HIS SEX LIFE

Atatürk's love life was far from boring, and over the course of his lifetime, he had many lovers. He took up with the most famous of these, Fikriye Hanim—a dead ringer for silent movie actress Theda Bara—while he was starting out as a soldier, but Atatürk dumped her in favor of feminist Latife Hanim, who soon became his wife. Upon hearing the news of her ex's quick nuptials, Fikriye committed suicide. Two years later, Atatürk and Hanim divorced, though he is reported to have regretted the decision.

→ WHY HE MATTERS

The bold social reforms of Turkey's first president proved hugely important, not just to the country he founded, but to all Arab states. In a

ADOPTION OF CHILDREN

After his divorce, Atatürk began adopting children at a rate that would make Brangelina blush. In total, he adopted seven daughters and one son, and kept two other children under his protection without officially adopting them.

→ Daughters:

1. Afet (Inan)
2. Sabiha (Gökcen)
3. Fikriye
4. Ülkü
5. Nebile
6. Rukiye
7. Zehra

→ Son:

8. Mustafa (named after himself, duh)

→ Protected children

9. Abdurrahim
10. Ihsan

short span of time, he transformed a conservative theocracy into a nation primed for Western-style democracy.

→ BEST FEATURE: **His diplomacy.**

Atatürk learned to separate his private life from his public acts. While women were literally killing themselves over him, he focused on maintaining a ferocious military presence and bringing Turkish law into the twentieth century—now that's multitasking.

→ HEAT FACTOR: **It's hard not to love a powerful man, and Atatürk grabbed all the power for himself.**

With his impeccable posture, neatly trimmed mustache, and dapper military garb, Atatürk cut a dashing figure, but his headache-inducing love life and reported drinking problem are a little bit of a turnoff. However, a legacy of legendary diplomacy might just sway things in his favor.

QUOTABLES

"Turkey would never want to see its founding father, which it sees as a holy person, be portrayed as a person with human weaknesses."

The Turkish Daily News

"The name of Atatürk brings to mind the historic accomplishments of one of the great men of this century, his inspired leadership of the Turkish People, his perceptive understanding of the modern world and his boldness as a military leader."

John F. Kennedy

"Victory is for those who can say 'Victory is mine'. Success is for those who can begin saying 'I will succeed' and say 'I have succeeded' in the end."

Mustafa Kemal Atatürk

PABLO PICASSO

"Love is the greatest refreshment in life."

VITAL STATS

YEARS: *1881 – 1973*

COUNTRY OF ORIGIN: *Spain*

AREA OF INFLUENCE:
Visual Arts

STYLE OF SEDUCTION:
Livin' large, in every sense

№ 21

An artist who worked in multiple mediums, including painting and sculpture, Pablo Picasso helped found Cubism, a revolutionary new style that changed the art world forever. He is widely regarded as one of the greatest and most influential artists of the twentieth century.

→ PICASSO'S LIFE STORY

Picasso's father was a painter and art teacher, and his mother was a devout Catholic. The couple's combination of creativity and piety gave Picasso quite a mouthful of a name that referred to both relatives and saints: Pablo Diego José Francisco de Paula Juan Nepomuceno María de los Remedios Cipriano de la Santísima Trinidad Clito Ruíz y Picasso. He used his father's surname, Ruiz, or his mother's, Picasso, on his earliest artwork, but started using Picasso exclusively around 1901.

With a father who painted and taught art for a living, it's little wonder Picasso became keenly interested in art at an early age—his first word was reportedly *piz*, a shorter version of *lápiz*, the Spanish word for "pencil." When his sister, Conchita, contracted diphtheria at the age of seven, young Picasso made a bargain with God: If his sister was spared, he would never pick up a paintbrush again. When she died, he blamed both God and himself. He decided that God had released him from his terrible bargain and set out to be an artist.

In 1895, the family moved to Barcelona, and Picasso began attending La Lajona, an academy of fine arts, to nurture his budding painting skills. A few years later, just before he turned nineteen, Picasso moved to Paris where he put on his first exhibition. It was there that he entered what became known as his Blue Period, creating blue-tinged and melancholic paintings. After painting incredible pieces including *Blue Nude* and *The Old Guitarist*, Picasso met his girlfriend, Fernande Olivier, started feeling better, and began using lots of red. The next few years were known as his Rose Period.

Around 1906, his work began moving further away from portraying the world in a traditional, representational manner. Instead, he began making paintings that broke down and analyzed form. The most famous of these early works is likely *Les Demoiselles d'Avignon*, which depicts a group of women as angular beige shapes instead of realistic female bodies. He continued working in this style and, along with the French artist Georges Braque, invented cubism, an abstract, avant-garde style that depicts objects from multiple viewpoints. Picasso continued to experiment with the cubist style for the rest of his career. *Guernica*, his 1937 cubist painting of the bombing of a Basque village during the Spanish Civil War, is considered the most famous work of his career.

Picasso remained an influential artist for the rest of his life, inspiring modern painters to push the limits of how they represented the world around them. He died at the age of ninety-one in France.

COMMUNISM

An outspoken member of the Communist Party, Picasso ascribed his involvement to a childhood spent in poverty. His political sensibilities did not stop him from painting an extremely unflattering portrait of Josef Stalin upon his death, one so ugly that it enraged the Soviet Union. Picasso brushed off the incident, however, saying that everyone had a right to react to his work in their own way.

✦ THE STORY OF HIS SEX LIFE

First, the numbers: two wives, three baby mamas, four kids, and countless lovers—this was a man who, by all accounts, had a lot of sex. Here are five of the women who made the biggest impact on his life and work.

Fernande Olivier: Picasso's first real girlfriend, a Frenchwoman, made him happy enough to exit his Blue Period and enter his Rose Period. They stayed together for seven years, during which time she remained married to sculptor Gaston de Labaume.

Olga Khokhlova: Picasso's first wife was a Russian ballerina and the daughter of a Russian colonel. He was intrigued by her Russian heritage but not excited by her personality, as he was used to spending time with bohemians, prostitutes, and progressive artists. They had a son together named Paulo.

Marie-Thérèse Walter: Marie-Thérèse was only seventeen when Picasso met her. She became Picasso's mistress while he was still married to Khokhlova, and he rented her an apartment across the street from the one he shared with his wife. Picasso and Marie-Thérèse had a daughter together. Marie-Thérèse, heartbroken after Picasso's death, hanged herself.

Françoise Gilot: Picasso and Gilot began their relationship when he was sixty-three; she was forty years his junior. They were together for ten years and had two children before she became fed up with his philandering.

Jacqueline Roque: Picasso married his second wife when he was seventy-nine and she was thirty-four. He painted portraits of her almost exclusively from the time they married until his death.

⇗ WHY HE MATTERS

Picasso is among the most famous and important artists of all time. Like very few artists in history, he was widely appreciated during his lifetime, and his work engaged the tumultuous events around him. His sculpture and paintings influenced more than just the field of visual art: Works of dance, literature, and film have all been touched by Picasso.

⇗ BEST FEATURE: **His unique vision.**

Picasso was not a conventionally handsome man, but he had more girlfriends than paintbrushes. He was a passionate lover and a forthright communicator, plus he had the power to immortalize his lovers forever in

lover "du jour"

fabulous (though not always flattering) paintings. His artistic sensibilities made him see the world, and relationships, a little differently than most.

⇗ HEAT FACTOR: **Picasso was an artistic genius who broke the rules both on the canvas and in the bedroom.**

Pro: Picasso's genius changed twentieth-century art. **Con:** He went through women like Kleenex. Does the idea of your portrait hanging on a museum wall outweigh the likelihood your partner will leave you for a seventeen-year-old? That's up to you.

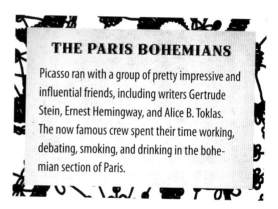

THE PARIS BOHEMIANS

Picasso ran with a group of pretty impressive and influential friends, including writers Gertrude Stein, Ernest Hemingway, and Alice B. Toklas. The now famous crew spent their time working, debating, smoking, and drinking in the bohemian section of Paris.

IN HIS OWN WORDS

"Art is a lie that makes us realize the truth."

"Ah, good taste! What a dreadful thing! Taste is the enemy of creativeness."

"The purpose of art is washing the dust of daily life off our souls."

COCO CHANEL

"There is only one Chanel."

VITAL STATS

YEARS: *1883 – 1971*

COUNTRY OF ORIGIN: *France*

AREAS OF INFLUENCE:
Fashion, Style

STYLE OF SEDUCTION:
Lookin' and talkin' fresh

No.
22

Coco Chanel was a trailblazing style icon whose belief that "luxury must be comfortable, otherwise it is not luxury" led to enormous changes in women's fashion and in the fashion industry as a whole.

➔ CHANEL'S LIFE STORY

Born Gabrielle Bonheur Chanel, Coco Chanel's life was literally a rags-to-riches story. Her father earned a small income by trading cheap bonnets and aprons at the markets, but the family consistently struggled to make ends meet. Chanel's mother died when Gabrielle was still just a child, and of the five children, the boys were sent off to work, while Gabrielle was left with her sister on the steps of a Catholic convent.

Though the living conditions were pretty bonkers, Mademoiselle Chanel made the most of her situation, asking the nuns to teach her how to sew. In the end, though, she wasn't a convent kind of girl. She earned the nickname "Coco" while performing in a cabaret. The name may have been a reference to the French word *cocotte*, meaning "kept woman." At the cabaret, in the presence of admiring patrons sporting some serious ice, Chanel first got a taste for the opulent displays of wealth she pursued for the rest of her life. When the seamstress later flourished into an icon, she was embarrassed by the pretty pauper image and rewrote these early years of her history, claiming to have been raised by spinster aunts in an idealized version of the typical, well-adjusted household.

Unfortunately, Coco had one of those "don't quit your day job" singing voices, and she relied instead on her "kept woman" skills (read between the lines) to fund her first shop, which opened in Paris in 1910. Her little hole-in-the-wall establishment was filled with simple but chic hats and knickknacks and was, at the time, the closest approximation to what today we would call a boutique. The House of Chanel slowly began to generate significant revenue. No longer financially dependent on schmoozy bankers, the couturier began selling dresses to match the store's established aesthetic—no corsets needed, just easy, breezy cuts that flowed over the body. Her collections first caught the eye of ballet dancers, who were often kept women themselves, which led to

No Corsets Needed!

the attention of businessmen who wished to carry her sophisticated and unfussy styles in their shops as well.

Coco Chanel is credited with the invention of countless fashion trends that have lasted through the decades, setting the industry standard for high-society women. The ubiquitous wrap dress, the Chanel suit, the quilted Chanel bag sporting the CC logo, little black dresses, and costume jewelry are all attributed to this mastermind. Anticipating war in 1939, she closed her shop, but reopened in 1953 after becoming alarmed by the restrictive fashions coming from places like Dior. Throughout her life, she sought to create couture that was tailored to real female bodies.

In 1971, Coco Chanel died in her sleep—at the Hotel Ritz.

✦ THE STORY OF HER SEX LIFE

Coco Chanel never married—I mean, when would she have the time? That's not to say she was too busy to have a love life, though. Without the means to earn a high enough income on her own, the style idol reeled in a series of financiers through love affairs, and then—voilà!—she was able to start her own business. Coincidence? History says not so much. Upon discovering that they were being pitted against each other to the benefit of Coco's bottom line, playboys Etienne Balsan and Boy Capel amicably agreed to split the funds that she needed.

31 RUE CAMBON

The address of one of Chanel's very first boutiques, 31 Rue Cambon, was also a fairly, um, unusual residence. How unusual was it? Let us count the ways . . .

➜ **Mirrors.** Notoriously fond of both gazing at herself and spying on others without being seen, the designer covered the walls of her flat with dozens upon dozens of mirrors.

➜ **Doors.** Never one to allow barriers between herself and others, Chanel was philosophically opposed to doors. Instead, she placed translucent Chinese screens in the entryways in the hopes, according to one archivist, that her guests would simply never leave.

➜ **Sleeping arrangements.** The flat contained absolutely zero bedrooms. Coco always slept across the street at the Ritz.

In the course of her romantic acrobatics, Chanel became entangled with the Duke of Westminster—that is, until allegations surfaced about her being a potential World War I spy. Though our girl was most definitely sleeping with the enemy, she managed to avoid consequences by sleeping with the home team, too.

WHY SHE MATTERS

Women the whole world over have reason to be grateful to Coco Chanel. It's due to her innovations that women no longer need to wear pounds of wool and suffocating undergarments to look presentable. She was the first designer to use knit jersey fabric in formal wear, and her suits were not only well cut but comfortable. The influence of Chanel's brand of minimalist design can be seen in both contemporary fashion, from the Armani runway to Nike running gear, and fine art.

BEST FEATURE: **Her integrity.**

Even at the peak of her game, Coco Chanel was a no-frills kind of girl, often dressing in all black and in a noticeably childlike manner, with straw hats and unadorned shifts that wouldn't weigh her down. Her fashion philosophy let the woman wear the clothes, rather than the clothes wearing the woman, and she designed her dresses to showcase the natural shape of the babe underneath.

HEAT FACTOR: **Nothing's hotter than the next big thing—and that's what Coco Chanel was. (It's also what she created for women throughout the twentieth century.)**

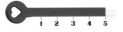

This lady-turned-logo rocked girly chic like it was her job—because it was. She broke the hearts of some of the most esteemed members of British high society—politicians, soldiers, bankers, poets, you name it. Nor did she ever let this long line of men slow her down. Coco Chanel knew what she wanted and got what she wanted, with cigarette in hand—and then she kept on moving.

If you're looking for lasting love, you're knocking at the wrong door, but if you want to run with the cool kids and look like a star, Coco's the one for you (that is, if you're the one for her).

IN HER OWN WORDS

"Fashion is not simply a matter of clothes. Fashion is in the air, born upon the wind. One intuits it. It is in the sky and on the road."

"The most courageous act is still to think for yourself. Aloud."

"I don't care what you think about me. I don't think about you at all."

"My life didn't please me, so I created my life."

T.E. LAWRENCE

"Lawrence of Arabia"

VITAL STATS

YEARS: *1888– 1935*

COUNTRY OF ORIGIN: *Wales*

AREA OF INFLUENCE: *Warfare*

STYLE OF SEDUCTION:
Explorin' new territory

Nº 23

Archaeologist and explorer at heart, Lawrence of Arabia was lauded for commanding the Great Arab Revolt against the Turks during World War I. He was a real-life Indiana Jones.

➤ LAWRENCE'S LIFE STORY

Lawrence's father, Sir Thomas Chapman, fled Ireland (and his wife) with his children's governess, moved to Wales, and started a second family known as the Lawrences. Thomas Edward—the future Lawrence of Arabia—was their second of five sons. After moving around for a while, the fledgling family landed in Oxford, where young Lawrence attended both secondary school and Oxford University. While studying military history, he took a school trip to Syria, where he embarked on a thousand-mile walking tour of the castles of the Crusaders. It was there he realized his passion for archaeology.

After graduation, he returned to Syria to work on an archaeological dig. As the protégé of noted archaeologist D.G. Hogarth, Lawrence traveled extensively through the Middle East, drawing up maps of uncharted territory.

At the start of World War I, Lawrence worked as a civilian in the map department of London's war office. His expertise in Arab matters proved too valuable to keep him behind a desk, and he was assigned to the British Army in Cairo. The British sensed that the Turks would join the Central powers, so it was in their best interest to align with the Arabs and help them escape from under Turkish rule. Lawrence fought alongside Emir Feisal, the leader of the Arab revolt, waging guerilla warfare against Turkish forces. At the end of the war, Western leaders ultimately ceded Syria to the French, frustrating Lawrence, who had wanted Syria to become an independent state. Lawrence, very disappointed at the time, attempted to retire, but Churchill called him back into military service as an adviser on the creation of a pro-Arab state in the Middle East. When Emir Feisal was appointed the leader of Iraq, Lawrence was at last satisfied.

After this victory of Middle Eastern independence, Lawrence attempted to continue his military service, but the fame he'd gained during World War I kept him hounded by the press. He retired early to the English countryside and died in a motorcycle crash at the age of forty-six. He just never slowed down.

◈ The Story of His Sex Life

T.E. Lawrence was never romantically linked with anybody, and it was speculated he might have been asexual. But a document released in 2002 showed that the Royal Air Force had paid him a marriage allowance for the last ten years of his life. The identity of this woman remains a mystery.

◈ Why He Matters

Lawrence brought the West's attention to the plight of Arabs in the Middle East, an area of the world that had previously been a romantic mystery to most Westerners. Plus, his writings on the theory of guerilla warfare influenced British military strategists for years to come.

VEGETARIANISM

During college, T.E. Lawrence subsisted on fruits and veggies, eggs, milk, and cake. While traveling in France, he offended his meat-eating hosts by remarking with satisfaction on the unusually high vegetable content in one of his meals. There's no record of Lawrence's reason for abstaining from meat, however. He also steered clear of drugs and alcohol.

LEAVING HIS STAMP

For a brief period of eight years in the early twentieth century, there existed a region west of Saudi Arabia called the Kingdom of Hejaz. As we know, Lawrence of Arabia was obsessed with all things Arab and decided to create something tangible that would encapsulate and honor the place. Upon the kingdom's inception in 1916, the first ruler, Sharif Hussein ibn Ali, requested that Lawrence create a design for the first three stamps that would represent the territory. When these stamps, which had an abstract scrolling pattern, turned up many years later, they were placed in the Royal Philatelic Collection in St. James' Palace, London.

After the kingdom folded in 1924, the stamps became difficult to track down and, thus, incredibly valuable. Because of this, the stamps were moved in 2010 to a higher-profile display at the Guildhall Art Gallery in London.

◈ Best feature: **His perfect pairing of brains and brawn.**

The thought of a trained archaeologist going on to lead guerilla armies to fight for freedom would make anybody swoon. While some may scoff at his total disregard of military regulations and lack of respect for authority, we call it moxie. He was a pretty good writer, too. To wit: "The dreamers by day are dangerous men, for they may act their dreams with open eyes to make it possible," he wrote in his memoir.

✦ HEAT FACTOR: **Hotter than midday in the desert, Lawrence of Arabia was a gorgeous, intelligent adventurer—a total catch.**

1 2 3 4 5

Photographers often caught this ruggedly handsome gent in traditional Arab garb staring straight ahead with his piercing gaze. How could anyone resist? When he wasn't advocating for the Arabs or parsing the fineries of guerilla warfare, he relaxed by translating Greek poetry. Meow!

piercing gaze

QUOTABLES

"The world looks with some awe upon a man who appears unconcernedly indifferent to home, money, comfort, rank, or even power and fame. The world feels not without a certain apprehension, that here is someone outside its jurisdiction; someone before whom its allurements may be spread in vain; someone strangely enfranchised, untamed, untrammelled by convention, moving independent of the ordinary currents of human action."

Winston Churchill

"The untidiest officer in the British Army."

fellow British soldier Ronald Storrs

"With hindsight, it is easy to see why a slim, self-effacing Englishman named Thomas Edward Lawrence became one of this century's most ballyhooed celebrities. Out of the appalling carnage of World War I—the mud-caked anonymity of the trenches, the hail of mechanized death that spewed from machine guns and fell from airplanes—there emerged a lone Romantic, framed heroically against the clean desert sands of Arabia."

Time writer Paul Gray

JIM THORPE

"the greatest athlete in the world"

No. 24

Jim Thorpe was the greatest athlete of his time and one of the first celebrities in American sports culture. Despite being dismissed and mocked on account of his American Indian roots, he used his accomplishments on the field to help found the NFL and pave the way for minority athletes everywhere.

➔ THORPE'S LIFE STORY

While we do know that James Francis Thorpe was born in a cabin in the Indian territory on the Oklahoma frontier, further details concerning his birth and heritage are foggy and often disputed. He was raised by devoutly Catholic parents as a Sac and Fox Indian with the name Wa-Tho-Huk, loosely translated as "Bright Path." In 1904, he attended the Carlisle Industrial Indian School in southern Pennsylvania with the goal of learning a trade and making a living.

In 1907, the 178-pound Thorpe was persuaded to try out for the football team by Coach Glenn S. (Pop) Warner, and a year later, he expanded his interests to include jumping and hurdling for the track team. Despite turning heads with his unprecedented speed, the budding athlete yearned for home and was only sweet-talked back to school by Coach Warner's promise of Olympic prospects. That promise proved reliable, for at just twenty-four years old, Thorpe did laps (sans Dramamine) aboard the ship that carried him and the rest of the United States team to the 1912 Olympics in Sweden. The unstoppable wunder-kind ran circles around his competition and set records that would prove unbeatable for decades to come, winning both the pentathlon and what was then considered the most difficult athletic event, the decathlon.

Upon returning to the United States, the newly galvanized American hero scored 25 touchdowns and 198 points for Carlisle's football team and rode his wave of fame through the following year— at which point it all came crashing down. Discovered

to have been paid for playing two seasons of semiprofessional baseball prior to competing in the games (considered a conflict of interest in the early 1900s), Thorpe was stripped of his gold medals (which weren't restored until 1982, well after his death). What a career setback, right? No way, not for Thorpe, who went on to play professional baseball and football concurrently for various teams, as well as help found the American Professional Football Association in 1920, which would later become the NFL. Unfortunately, after organizing his own pro team, the Canton (Ohio) Bulldogs, his life began to fall apart. He was an alcoholic, but despite his physical decline, Thorpe was the only one in his family to enjoy anything like old age. He survived well into his sixth decade and spent the remainder of his days in California doing odd jobs like digging ditches and keeping out the riffraff as a bar bouncer. After a brief stint as a marine in World War II, the former gold medalist died of a heart attack alone in his trailer in 1953. He was broke.

⇒ THE STORY OF HIS SEX LIFE

As in so much of his personal narrative, little is known about Jim Thorpe's love life—only rumors. He wed three times, an uncommon occurrence in the first half of the twentieth century, and that fact alone set the gossip mill ablaze with conjecture. After his wins at the Olympics, his celebrity, coupled with some liquor, and tripled with his good looks, made for a dangerous brew. That is, at least according to his first two wives, Iva Miller and Freeda Kirkpatrick. His third wife, Patty Askew, left him after his health began to suffer. He had children with all three of his wives, and his youngest son, Jack Thorpe, eventually became principal chief of the Sac and Fox Indians. Thorpe was a fighter

more than a lover, pulling such stunts as dumping a police officer upside down in a garbage can.

⇒ WHY HE MATTERS

Though athletes of late have broken Thorpe's formerly unbeatable records, he brought athletic achievement to the next level, never needing to specialize in one sport in order to nurture his game (and showing up teammates who had followed fancy fitness regimens since childhood). The original barefoot running enthusiast, Thorpe showed the world that old-school training methods—running twenty miles home from school at his father's insistence, to give just one example—could be translated into real-world success.

Paying little attention to either critics or spectators, Jim Thorpe put so much of himself into his game that a tiny town in northeastern Pennsylvania, not too far from Carlisle, was named in his honor. Called the greatest athlete of the first half of the twentieth century by the Associated Press, he was much more than an athlete. He was a legend—*and* the man behind the National Football League.

⇗ BEST FEATURE: **Between his biceps and his triceps and his twenty-four-inch thighs (yikes!), it's kind of hard to choose.**

Jim Thorpe was a world-record beating athlete who left the competition wondering, "How does he do it?" But in a pre-steroids world, answers to that question were harder to come by. He was simply the greatest athlete alive.

⇗ HEAT FACTOR: **He never failed to torch the competition.**

Unfortunately, big Jim Thorpe didn't really respect anyone but big Jim Thorpe. And unless your name was "Football," he generally had bigger fish to fry. His nearly pious relationship with sports left little room for courtship, and his legendary physique meant he rarely had to try.

QUOTABLES

"Nobody was in his class. If you look at old pictures of him he looks almost modern. He's cut. He doesn't look soft like the other guys did back then. He looks great."

Olympic historian Bill Mallon

"He was the best natural athlete ever. No matter what sport he turned to, he was a magnificent performer. He had all the strength, speed and coordination of the finest players plus incredible stamina. His memory should be kept for what it deserves—that of the greatest all around athlete of our time."

The New York Times

"Sir, you are the greatest athlete in the world."

King Gustaf V of Sweden at the 1912 Olympic Games

DUKE KAHANAMOKU

"the father of modern surfing"

VITAL STATS

YEARS: *1890 – 1968*

COUNTRY OF ORIGIN:
The Kingdom of Hawaii

AREA OF INFLUENCE: *Athletics*

STYLE OF SEDUCTION:
*Doin' laps around
the competition*

No. 25

A s a world-championship swimmer, Duke Kahanamoku drew international attention to the territory of Hawaii. He then used his popularity as a gold medalist to bring the Hawaiian tradition of surfing to the wider world.

→ KAHANAMOKU'S LIFE STORY

Duke Kahanamoku was born in Honolulu, Hawaii. The first son of nine children, Duke Paoa Kahinu Mokoe Hulikohola Kahanamoku was named after his father, a police officer who had been born during the Duke of Edinburgh's first visit to Hawaii and named after the visiting dignitary. At the time of Duke Junior's birth, Hawaii was in shambles after a hundred years of interference from missionaries and explorers, its native culture nearly destroyed. During Kahanamoku's childhood, the Hawaiian monarchy was overthrown by U.S. military forces, and the former kingdom was annexed as a territory.

A child of privilege, Kahanamoku was largely unaware of the turmoil going on around him. He spent his time surfing and swimming instead. As he matured, he developed a physique perfectly suited for his hobbies: Standing six feet tall and weighing 190 pounds, Kahanamoku was lean and muscular. His size thirteen feet gave him built-in flippers.

Just before his twenty-first birthday, Kahanamoku competed in a swimming competition at the Amateur Athletic Union of Hawaii, breaking one world record and matching another; his time in the one-hundred-yard freestyle was 4.6 seconds faster than the previous world champion's. Amateur Athletic Union officials thought his times were a fluke, so the local AAU raised the money to send Kahanamoku to compete on the mainland and prove that he could break the records there, too. In his first competition at a meet in Chicago, he won the fifty- and one-hundred-yard freestyles once again. He won the Olympic pretrials

in Philadelphia later that year, and went on to join the 1912 Olympic team. At the Stockholm Olympics, he and American Indian track star Jim Thorpe raised the visibility of nonwhite U.S. athletes. Kahanamoku competed for the next twelve years and won his final Olympic gold medal in Paris in 1924 at the age of thirty-four.

During his run as an Olympic athlete, Kahanamoku used his fame as a platform to preach the gospel of surfing around the world. He trained surfers from New York to Australia, showing them how to make boards and catch waves. People loved the freedom of riding the waves, and what was once a little-known sport became an international sensation.

When Kahanamoku retired as an Olympic athlete, he became a film actor. His Hollywood career lasted twenty-eight years and included roles as a pirate, a lifeguard, a Hawaiian chief, and even a role alongside the great John Wayne. His good looks, athletic achievement, and Hollywood ties made him the unofficial spokesperson of Hawaii. He took visiting celebrities like Shirley Temple, Groucho Marx, and Babe Ruth to the then remote Waikiki Beach, helping make it into the tourist hot spot it is today.

After his film career ended, Kahanamoku returned to Hawaii full time. Fame had left him unprepared for the stress of supporting himself, and he had to take a job managing a pair of gas stations. He then followed in his father's footsteps and became the sheriff of Honolulu, a job he held for twenty-six years. Duke's days of fame weren't totally behind him, however, as he went on to endorse both a surfing championship and a line of Hawaiian shirts. Duke Kahanamoku died of a heart attack at the age of seventy-seven. A memorial statue of him posing with a surfboard stands at Waikiki Beach.

⟶ THE STORY OF HIS SEX LIFE

Duke Kahanamoku stayed single for most of his public life but married Nadine Alexander in 1940. The couple didn't have any children together and remained married until the end of Duke's life.

⟶ WHY HE MATTERS

In addition to being called the "Father of Modern Surfing" and one of the greatest athletes of his time, Kahanamoku became a world champion just as Hawaii was shaking off years of colonial oppression and reinventing itself as part of the modern West. By representing people of color on the world stage, he helped show that colonized people had a place in the global discussion.

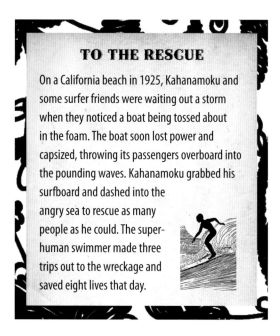

TO THE RESCUE

On a California beach in 1925, Kahanamoku and some surfer friends were waiting out a storm when they noticed a boat being tossed about in the foam. The boat soon lost power and capsized, throwing its passengers overboard into the pounding waves. Kahanamoku grabbed his surfboard and dashed into the angry sea to rescue as many people as he could. The super-human swimmer made three trips out to the wreckage and saved eight lives that day.

↯ BEST FEATURE: **His easy confidence.**

For all his accomplishments, Kahanamoku was by no means self-absorbed. At the Stockholm Olympics he tied the world record for the hundred-meter freestyle during a heat but didn't show up to the final. Teammates searched all over for him, finding him under a bridge, dead asleep. He woke up, apologized, and won the race.

Kahanamoku's confidence extended beyond the pool, helping him tackle extreme career transitions from Olympian, to actor, to gas station attendant, to sheriff. In the face of a challenge, he never blinked.

↯ HEAT FACTOR: **He may not have walked on water, but he did pretty much everything else.**

More than just your average beach bum, Kahanamoku showed his swimming and surfing skills off to the world. Tall and tan with chiseled muscles and excellent bone structure, Kahanamoku could surf his way into anyone's heart. Add to that physical perfection a whole lot of talent and perseverance, and you've got yourself one Hawaiian hunk.

— hunk

QUOTABLES

"Duke was a man of great virtue and spiritual worth. The most valuable of all was his humility. He wholly believed that a human being's greatest value is in the worth of their soul, not their pocketbook."

1968 world surfing champion Fred Hemmings

"Duke Kahanamoku of Honolulu is described as a wonder at 100 yards. [Jamison Handy of Chicago] describes Kahanamoku as a giant, ebony-skinned native about 20 years old, standing over six feet in stockings, weighing about 190 pounds, and a magnificent specimen of manhood, straight, well-muscled and perfectly formed. He . . . goes through the water with shoulders high above the surface, moving at fast speed."

The New York Times

"Brother Duke slept 99 percent of his time. He could sleep while he was sitting there talking to you. And I always thought that was what made him a great swimmer. He was clear in the head."

Duke's brother, Sergeant Kahanamoku

BESSIE COLEMAN

"Queen Bess"

VITAL STATS

YEARS: *1892 – 1926*
COUNTRY OF ORIGIN: *USA*
AREA OF INFLUENCE: *Aviation*
STYLE OF SEDUCTION:
Flyin' high

Elizabeth "Bessie" Coleman made her own way in the world, regardless of the odds stacked against her. She achieved an education despite limited resources, learned new skills when her progress stagnated, and eventually took to the skies as the first African American woman to pilot a plane.

→ COLEMAN'S LIFE STORY

Atlanta, Texas, was not a friendly place for African Americans at the turn of the twentieth century—not a friendly place at all. But this was where Bessie Coleman was forced to grow up (fast) among a family of fifteen. When her father set out for Indian Territory (he was part American Indian) in order to find some relief, her brothers didn't take long to follow suit, and Bess was left to raise her younger sisters while her mom made ends meet as a housecleaner. In the limited amount of "free" time available to her, Coleman learned to read and snuck off to the local library to peruse *Uncle Tom's Cabin* as well as books depicting the lives of black leaders.

Set on achieving an education against all odds, she went back to her tiny schoolhouse once her sisters were old enough to take care of themselves and then attended a vocational school in Oklahoma, until she ran out of money for tuition. Fed up with what seemed like a dead-end life in a dead-end town, Coleman hopped on a train to the Windy City, where her brothers had wound up as well. Upon arriving, she enrolled in beauty school and found work as a manicurist for various well-to-do types, including one of the first black American millionaires, Robert Abbott, who was then serving as publisher of the African American newspaper the *Chicago Defender*. After trimming the activist's nails, the two developed a close friendship, and she regaled the older man with tales of her brothers' experiences in World War I and fantastical feats of the war pilots in France. With encouragement and some financial help from Abbott, Coleman studied the language of love—French—and made her way to Europe to do what no woman in the States had accomplished: obtain a license to fly. After seven months in the cockpit of a French Nieuport Type 82, she did it. Back in the United States in 1922, she landed a spot in an air show performing flips and whirligigs.

A year after surviving a near-fatal crash before a show in Los Angeles, Coleman took to the skies to test her plane before a show in Florida. Adjusting her seat belt for a better view of the landscape, she was jolted out of the cockpit in a freak accident when the plane shuddered suddenly and she was catapulted to her death. She was thirty-four years old.

✦ The Story of Her Sex Life

Few details about Bessie Coleman's love life are public knowledge. She was a press darling whose chosen profession made her a point of focus in a boys-only crowd. Publicly, however, Brave Bessie had no significant other to speak of.

✦ Why She Matters

The first African American regardless of gender to receive a license to fly, Queen Bess didn't let the conventions of the time affect her self-worth and instead focused solely on achieving her vision. As a black woman, she had two strikes against her. But by taking her education into her own hands and seeking out those who would support her—traveling in blacks-only railcars the whole way—she became an inspiration not just to minorities but to anyone encountering obstacles while chasing a dream.

Coleman's success as a full-fledged aviatrix performing feats of flight did not go unacknowl-edged. Founded three years after her death by William J. Powell, the Bessie Coleman Aero Club was named by Powell to honor "a pioneer who I think well deserves the honor." The flying school hosted the first all-black air show in Chicago in 1931 with over 15,000 spectators and inspired the launch of several smaller organizations across the country dedicated to supporting the goals of young African Americans through flight.

The countless testaments to this pilot's legacy include a street named Bessie Coleman Drive in Chicago, an annual organized flight over her grave in Lincoln Cemetery, and the founding of a national aviation club for black women in 1977.

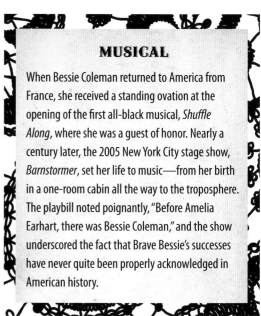

MUSICAL

When Bessie Coleman returned to America from France, she received a standing ovation at the opening of the first all-black musical, *Shuffle Along*, where she was a guest of honor. Nearly a century later, the 2005 New York City stage show, *Barnstormer*, set her life to music—from her birth in a one-room cabin all the way to the troposphere. The playbill noted poignantly, "Before Amelia Earhart, there was Bessie Coleman," and the show underscored the fact that Brave Bessie's successes have never quite been properly acknowledged in American history.

⊹ BEST FEATURE: **Her courage.**

Bessie Coleman's success story is so seamless it is as though she had never encountered adversity along the way when, in reality, every step of real progress she achieved was in spite of a major obstacle in her path. The utter fearlessness that she displayed throughout her life—illegally learning to read, skipping town to travel the length of the United States by herself, moving to a country whose language she didn't speak—lends her an air of real nobility, hence her nickname "Queen Bess."

⊹ HEAT FACTOR: **She believed she could fly! And then she touched the sky! She's hotter than R. Kelly lyrics—and who among us can honestly say that?**

1 2 3 4 5

If Bessie Coleman has any faults, they're not easy to see. She never shied away from asking for help when she needed it, and this humility—together with relentless ambition and inspired spirit—makes us lifelong devotees.

QUOTABLES

"*We all shared Bessie's love for flying and went through the doors that she cracked open.*"

Cyrus C. Cassells Jr.

"*It was unusual enough for a Negro to fly a plane, but for a Negro woman to do such a thing, it came near to being a miracle. That Ms. Coleman was a petite and attractive person and a worthy person to have pioneered in such a field.*"

Chicago Defender editor Enoc P. Waters

"*Because of Bessie Coleman, we have overcome that which was worse than racial barriers. We have overcome the barriers within ourselves and dared to dream.*"

Lieutenant William J. Powell

"*There is reason to believe that the general public did not completely sense the size of her contribution to the achievements of the race as such.*"

Dallas Express editorial

DOROTHY PARKER

"a combination of Little Nell and Lady Macbeth"

VITAL STATS

YEARS: *1893 – 1967*

COUNTRY OF ORIGIN: *USA*

AREA OF INFLUENCE: *Literature*

STYLE OF SEDUCTION: *Drinkin' the boys under the table*

<table>
<tr><td>№ 27</td></tr>
</table>

Dorothy Parker was an immensely talented writer and cultural figure whose bon mots were the stuff of legend in mid-twentieth-century Manhattan. She also helped to hone the format and style of the *New Yorker* short story as we know it today.

→ PARKER'S LIFE STORY

Born Dorothy Rothschild, Parker was raised on the Upper West Side of Manhattan. By her early twenties, she was writing for magazines such as *Vogue* and *Vanity Fair*. While at *Vanity Fair* she and two other writers founded what *they* called "The Vicious Circle" but which became known as the Algonquin Round Table. The Round Table grew into a decade-long lunch appointment featuring a rotating cast of critics, writers, and outspoken creative types at the Algonquin Hotel, a few blocks from *Vanity Fair*'s New York offices. Among Parker's mischievous compatriots were cofounders Robert Benchley and Robert E. Sherwood, *New Yorker* editor Harold Ross, playwright George S. Kaufman, and women's rights activist Ruth Hale. The group gained fame for their merciless gossip, ultramodern cultural critiques, and verbal one-upmanship. They also served as a kind of hype machine, as they would broadcast their appreciation for each others' work outside the circle. A permanent

Round Table fixture, Parker gained special fame as the quickest (and most acerbic) wit at lunch.

When Round Table member Harold Ross founded the *New Yorker* in 1925, he hired Parker to review books as the "Constant Reader," and her verdicts had the power to make or break careers. Prior to joining the magazine, she'd been fired from *Vanity Fair* for reviews that were considered to be too harsh, but as the Constant Reader she was allowed free reign. She did not disappoint. Turned off by Winnie the Pooh's baby talk in A. A. Milne's *The House at Pooh Corner*, she ended her review simply, "Tonstant Weader Frowed Up."

Parker didn't slow down after the workday was over, and as a result she quickly made a name for herself at Manhattan's many speakeasies and saloons, even becoming a regular at an upscale brothel, Polly Adler's. After a stint in Hollywood, where two screenplays she collaborated on—*A Star is Born* and *Smash Up: The Story of a Woman*—garnered Oscar nominations, Parker returned home to New York. Sadly, she developed a dependence on alcohol and eventually became too ill to work. She died of a heart attack and was cremated. Before her death, she claimed she wanted her epitaph to read, "Excuse my dust."

⇢ THE STORY OF HER SEX LIFE

Though famous for her columns, short stories, poetry, and punch lines, Parker wasn't always lucky in love. She was involved in several emotionally devastating love affairs, attempted suicide on numerous occasions, and was married three different times (twice to the same man, actor Allan Campbell). Parker's first marriage was to stockbroker Edwin Pond Parker II, who provided her with a "nice, clean" name but quickly deserted her to serve in World War I. After meeting Campbell, she moved to Hollywood.

Campbell committed suicide in 1963.

⇢ WHY SHE MATTERS

Parker was one of the first crop of writers at the *New Yorker*, which has since become an American institution. While there, she established the "*New Yorker* story"—pieces under 7,000 words that had to be tight and cosmopolitan, and over which Parker herself served as judge, jury, and executioner.

⇢ BEST FEATURE: **Her serious wit.**

Parker was as cute as a button and hysterical to boot. She had the guts to leave her estate to Martin Luther King Jr., well before he was universally respected (see sidebar, facing page). Her sense of humor was her greatest asset, but she was also stylish, with a naturally tiny figure and large and lovely hazel eyes. Though she was always at the ready with a quip and a laugh, Parker was rarely photographed smiling, but occasionally instead cocked one dark, strong brow. No one escaped her examination, and few could resist her charm—dangerous as it was to be around. "Wit has truth in it," she once said. "Wisecracking is simply calisthenics with words."

cocked brow

➤ HEAT FACTOR: **Almost too hot to handle.**

Parker's biting sense of humor could be intimidating to some, but intoxicating to others. Though shallow about appearances (she coined the phrase "Men seldom make passes at girls who wear glasses"), she was a tireless advocate for civil rights throughout her life. Her spirit lives on to this day, and the Dorothy Parker Foundation was created in 1998 to pay homage to her works and general spunk. When caught at a saloon while on the *New Yorker*'s payroll, Parker claimed, "Someone else was using the pencil." In her obituary in the *New York Times*,

Parker was called both "deceptively sweet" and "a glittering, annihilating humorist."

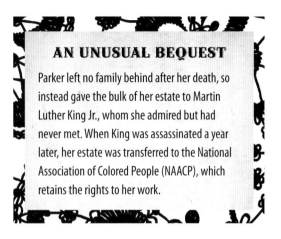

AN UNUSUAL BEQUEST

Parker left no family behind after her death, so instead gave the bulk of her estate to Martin Luther King Jr., whom she admired but had never met. When King was assassinated a year later, her estate was transferred to the National Association of Colored People (NAACP), which retains the rights to her work.

IN HER OWN WORDS

"I don't care what is written about me so long as it isn't true."

"I'm never going to accomplish anything; that's perfectly clear to me. I'm never going to be famous. My name will never be writ large on the roster of Those Who Do Things. I don't do anything. Not one single thing. I used to bite my nails, but I don't even do that anymore."

"I'd rather have a bottle in front of me, than a frontal lobotomy."

AMELIA EARHART

"Lady Lindy"

VITAL STATS

YEARS: *1897 – 1937*
COUNTRY OF ORIGIN: *USA*
AREA OF INFLUENCE: *Aviation*
STYLE OF SEDUCTION:
Flyin' solo

No. 28

People can change. For proof, just look to Amelia Earhart. When she was a little girl, she said airplanes were "not at all interesting," but she grew up to become a legendary pilot and the first woman to fly alone across the Atlantic Ocean.

→ EARHART'S LIFE STORY

Born to a prominent Kansas clan, young Amelia spent her days shooting rats with a rifle, building roller coasters, and longing for the day when she would become an executive—a lofty dream for a woman in those days. But fate had other plans for her. After graduating high school in the thick of World War I, Earhart trained as a nurse for the Red Cross and tended to wounded soldiers in Canada. She liked it so much she enrolled in Columbia University's pre-med program but dropped out a year later.

Earhart drifted to California, where her parents were living at the time. At an air show in Long Beach, she took a ride in a plane and, after she got a peek at the view from above, there was no going back. She threw herself into flying lessons and bought a banana-yellow biplane built for two that she christened *Canary*. She cut her hair, slept in her leather jacket, and made a name for herself as the first woman to rise fourteen thousand feet in the air.

When her family's fortune began to dwindle, Earhart moved to Boston to be closer to her sister. It was there, in 1928, that she was asked to fly across the Atlantic for the first time along with two men. After a New York ticker tape parade and a party with President Calvin Coolidge were held in her honor, she set about becoming a celebrity. Earhart lent her name to luggage lines and active wear and became an editor at *Cosmopolitan* magazine, using her platform to promote women in aviation. All the while, she engaged in acts of derring-do: racing, performing stunts, and flying pretty much all the time.

Charles Lindbergh had made his historic solo journey across the Atlantic in 1927, and Americans were curious to see if a woman could make the trip, too. Earhart achieved that dream and was the first woman to make the solo trip in 1932. In 1937, looking for something new, she was ready to circumnavigate the equator. It was something that no pilot had ever done (men had flown around the globe before but not at the equator). She took off from a Miami runway, and after a refueling stop in New Guinea she was never seen again. With just seven thousand miles left to her trip, but facing the most difficult leg of the journey, Earhart lost her radio signal. The last thing the Coast Guard heard her say was, "We are running north and south." The government spent $4 million searching for her but never found the plane or Earhart. The mystery surrounding her death lingers even today.

THE STORY OF HER SEX LIFE

Earhart met the publisher George P. Putnam when he offered to sponsor her trans-Atlantic flight. Three years (and several rejected proposals) later, Putnam finally won Earhart over, and the two were married. Earhart kept her maiden name and called her marriage a partnership with "dual control." Putnam often served as Earhart's publicist, organizing her events and arranging endorsement deals for her. His final act as Earhart's partner was writing and publishing her biography, *Soaring Wings*, which was released two years after her disappearance.

WHY SHE MATTERS

Amelia Earhart put the "dare" in daredevil. The boundaries she broke are ones that we take for granted today. Earhart embodies what women can achieve if they pursue their dreams and don't let anything stop them. Because of her, not even the sky is the limit.

BEST FEATURE: **Her spunkiness.**

In a letter that Amelia Earhart wrote to George Putnam, she summed up her feelings about flying: "I want to do it because I want to do it." Is there anything hotter than sheer, naked ambition and drive?

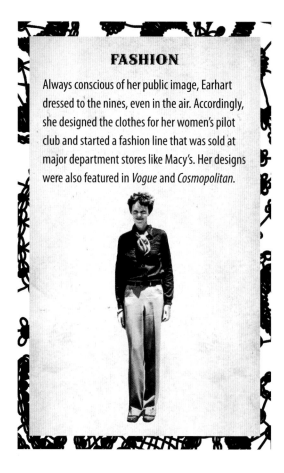

FASHION

Always conscious of her public image, Earhart dressed to the nines, even in the air. Accordingly, she designed the clothes for her women's pilot club and started a fashion line that was sold at major department stores like Macy's. Her designs were also featured in *Vogue* and *Cosmopolitan*.

✦ HEAT FACTOR: **The closer you are to the sun, the hotter things get. Amelia Earhart flew higher than pretty much anyone else.**

In addition to being a pioneering feminist and groundbreaking daredevil, Amelia Earhart was also blessed with cheekbones that could cut butter and hair that looked wonderful even when severely windblown.

THE FLYERCOASTER

As a young girl, Earhart was just as much of a visionary as she was in adulthood. After visiting the 1904 St. Louis World's Fair and witnessing the mechanics of a roller coaster, she and her sister decided to construct a mini version in their backyard, on the roof of a tool shed. At what was supposed to be the end of the ride (enabled in part by a healthy dose of grease), the brave young Earhart wasn't able to stop and went hurtling off the roof. Even then, you couldn't keep her from flying.

QUOTABLES

"There was this woman Amelia Earhart, who, when it was really hard, decided she was going to break all kinds of limits—social limits, gravity limits, distance limits. NASA may have said I couldn't go into space, but nobody was there to tell Amelia Earhart she couldn't do what she chose to do. Now it has been 75 years since she set out in that twin-engine Lockheed Electra to be the first pilot, man or woman, to fly around the world along the longest equatorial route. Her legacy resonates today for anyone, girls and boys, who dreams of the stars."

Hillary Clinton

"It is well documented that Amelia had freckles and disliked having them."

researcher Joe Cerniglia

"To Amelia Earhart, may she find her way!"

Jennifer Lawrence, in a toast at a party in Hollywood

ERNEST HEMINGWAY

a king among
men (and cats)

VITAL STATS

YEARS: *1899 – 1961*

COUNTRY OF ORIGIN: *USA*

AREA OF INFLUENCE: *Literature*

STYLE OF SEDUCTION:
*Sailin' boats, drinkin' whiskey,
shootin' game, fightin' fights,
and writin' manly sentences
from Miami to Madrid*

№ 29

H emingway was a writer. He was a man. He sailed boats, and when someone hit him, he hit back, hard. He hated adjectives and cuddling. He was a hunter, a fisherman, and an American. He was Ernest Hemingway.

→ HEMINGWAY'S LIFE STORY

Hemingway was born and raised in the Chicago suburbs. His father and mother, a physician and a musician, respectively, were fairly well-off, and by age four, the toddler alternated his time between playing the cello, hunting, and fishing. As a teenager, however, Hemingway ditched the classical instrument and doubled-down on the wilderness portion of the curriculum, and nature eventually became an important theme in his work.

While still a student, Hemingway began to flex his literary muscles as a journalist for his high school newspaper and for the school yearbook, *Tabula*. With those accomplishments—however modest—on his résumé, he was able to move and find work at the *Kansas City Star*, whose style guide played a major role in developing his voice as a writer: "Use short sentences. Use short first paragraphs. Use vigorous English."

In 1918, Hemingway left the States for Europe, which was then embroiled in World War I. He served as an ambulance driver and Red Cross volunteer in Italy, where he was wounded while on duty. In return for saving a fellow soldier's life, young Hemingway received the Italian Silver Medal of Bravery. Yet, not even six months in the hospital could slow him down, as he quickly fell in love with his caretaker, Agnes von Kurowsky. She agreed to marry him but then ran off with a less-vulnerable Italian officer. In all of his ensuing marriages (save the last), Hemingway would wind up abandoning his wife before she had a chance to abandon him. In a way, his advice to overcome writer's block paralleled his strategy for love: "The best way is always to stop when you are going good and when you know what will happen next. If you do that every day . . . you will never be stuck."

While recovering at home from his war injuries, Hemingway began writing stories of loneliness—the isolation of the forests, the solitariness of soldiers in battle—and with that, his fiction career commenced. He also accepted a position at the *Toronto Star* in order to gain a real-world income, and eventually worked as a foreign correspondent in France, where he moved with his first wife, the redheaded Hadley Richardson. While reveling in both the grit and the glory of 1920s Paris, he secured a drinking partner in James Joyce, a proofreader in Ezra Pound, and a mentor in Gertrude Stein. After drinking deeply from the cup of life in Europe, the young couple moved back to Toronto in 1923, where Hadley gave birth to their first son while Ernest published his first book, a collection of stories called *Three Stories and Ten Poems*. Hemingway yearned for the quicker tempo of a big European city, however, and the couple soon returned to Paris—where they were then divorced.

Hemingway's wanderlust got a little out of hand during his second marriage to Pauline Pfeiffer. Together they went from Key West to Wyoming, Kansas City (where his second son was born), Cuba, East Africa, and finally the Caribbean, where he went on a self-guided boating tour. Soon after, he began covering the Spanish Civil War and World War II while simultaneously

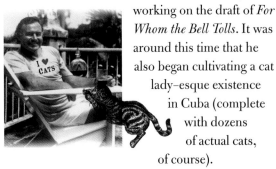

working on the draft of *For Whom the Bell Tolls*. It was around this time that he also began cultivating a cat lady–esque existence in Cuba (complete with dozens of actual cats, of course).

In 1954, Hemingway was falsely reported dead after surviving two plane crashes while on safari in Africa. His receipt of the Nobel Prize for literature in October of the same year was tainted, in his opinion, by the proximity of the two events. In a foreboding acceptance speech, Hemingway wrote of life as an author: "For he does his work alone and if he is a good enough writer he must face eternity, or the lack of it, each day." The curmudgeon spent much of the rest of his life bedridden with various alcohol-related ailments, such as liver disease and hypertension. In 1961, Hemingway followed in the tragic footsteps of his father, brother, and sister by committing suicide.

➔ THE STORY OF HIS SEX LIFE

A tryst in the City of Lights wouldn't be complete without a little romantic drama. Hemingway's time in Paris certainly had that, as his literary star was rising just as his marriage was falling apart— due in part to an affair with *Vogue* writer Pauline Pfeiffer.

In the style of every reality TV show there ever was, he later in life proposed to his third wife, Mary, while still married to his second wife, Martha. Hemingway wouldn't stand for panned reviews of both his latest relationship and his latest work, so—always an author first—he composed the draft of *The Old Man and the Sea* in a marathon eight weeks.

➔ WHY HE MATTERS

Though his reputation for boozing sometimes overshadows the legacy of his literature, Ernest

Hemingway was a Lost Generation (a phrase he borrowed from Gertrude Stein for one of the two epigraphs in *The Sun Also Rises*) novelist perhaps most notable for the high school English favorites *For Whom the Bell Tolls* and *The Old Man and the Sea*. Hemingway was seriously rolling in literary swag, winning the Pulitzer for fiction in 1953, then the Nobel Prize for literature in 1954. Indubitably in the "bad boy" category, the writer was a rugged veteran of two World Wars and three ex-wives, and he had a lifelong obsession with bullfighting. His wartime prose humanized the soldiers of World Wars I and II and is still read in classrooms today to better understand the turbulent history of this period.

→ BEST FEATURE: **His manliness.**

It may have been exaggerated in his work, but the overwhelming manliness of Hemingway's pursuits—fighting men, fighting bulls, catching fish, chasing submarines, writing about wars and brawls and brutality—did nothing to detract from the appeal of his square-jawed masculinity. He had his problems, his cats, his insecurities, and his exes, but he also had a real thirst for life and for thrilling experiences. For a good time, call Ernest Hemingway. Just don't marry him.

→ HEAT FACTOR: **Too hot for words—or for extraneous adjectives, anyway.**

He was a bombastic, insecure, bipolar man—but man, did he live a full life. A date with Ernest Hemingway was a date you wouldn't soon forget, but a marriage to the literary icon was much more problematic, as a rule. Still, in terms of sheer masculine handsomeness, he's hard to beat.

IN HIS OWN WORDS

"I love sleep. My life has the tendency to fall apart when I'm awake, you know?"

"There is nothing to writing. All you do is sit down at a typewriter and bleed."

"I drink to make other people more interesting."

"There's no one thing that's true. It's all true."

№ 30

First as a dancer, then as an actress, director, and producer, Leni Riefenstahl was always devoted to the arts. But no matter what the quality of her other work, she will be forever remembered most for her stylish, Nazi propaganda films.

⇥ RIEFENSTAHL'S LIFE STORY

Born Helene Bertha Amalie Riefenstahl in Berlin, the future filmmaker initially trained as a ballerina, making a name for herself as a modern dancer in the style of Isadora Duncan. After giving recitals throughout Germany, Riefenstahl made an initial foray into film as an actress. She starred in what were known as mountain films, pictures that emphasized the natural beauty of the German countryside. Her blonde bombshell looks and on-screen allure caused Hollywood directors to court her, but Riefenstahl rebuffed them—she wanted to direct.

In 1931, she formed her own production company and directed and starred in her first feature—a fairy tale called *The Blue Light*—the following year. While *The Blue Light* showed off Riefenstahl's talents for editing, lighting, and visual drama, it was her first documentary that would truly capture the world's attention. In 1934, she filmed the Nazi rally at Nuremberg, releasing the documentary under the title *The Triumph of the Will*. (Anyone who's caught footage of a shouting Hitler on the History Channel has seen at least part of Riefenstahl's most famous work.) Although the film is considered propaganda, Riefenstahl denied those claims until her death.

Hitler funded her next documentary *Olympia*, an extended study of the German physique. The film premiered at the dictator's forty-ninth birthday party. In spite of its upsetting origins, the film is considered a true work of art, as well as Riefenstahl's masterpiece. She toured the world to promote it but was shunned for her politics.

Adolf with Leni in *front* of the camera

After the Nazi regime fell, Riefenstahl was forced to leave Germany. She fled to France, where she was briefly imprisoned for her involvement with the Nazis. Thanks to her association with Hitler, her film career was kaput. She moved to Africa to try her hand as a photographer, releasing a series of highly acclaimed photographs of the Nuba, a

Sudanese tribe that paints their faces as if they were intricate masks. Looking for yet another artistic outlet, she took up underwater photography at age seventy. Riefenstahl died at the incredible age of one hundred and one.

✦ THE STORY OF HER SEX LIFE

Riefenstahl didn't settle down until later in life—much later. She was briefly married to a Nazi officer and was rumored to have had an affair with Hitler himself, but she denied this insinuation. Finally, on her hundred and first birthday, she married her off-and-on boyfriend of thirty-five years, cinematographer Horst Kettner, only two weeks before she died.

PAPA HEMINGWAY'S INFLUENCE

Riefenstahl developed an obsession with Sudan in 1955 after reading Hemingway's *Green Hills of Africa*. She lived there for two decades, taking still photographs and focusing in particular on the Nuba tribe. The Nuba people were isolated from the outside world, and much of their art revolved around self-presentation and deeply stylized masks. This was a good match for an artist who was always preoccupied with human physicality.

RIEFENSTAHL'S LONG CAREER

The reaction to her fascistic aesthetic and role as a leading filmmaker in Nazi Germany kept Leni Riefenstahl out of the public eye for years, but she made her comeback in a big way. In 2002, she became the first filmmaker over the age of one hundred to release a work. Her forty-five-minute documentary *Underwater Impressions* encompassed close to a half a life's worth of images from the depths of various bodies of water. (And get this—the soundtrack for the short piece was written by the same guy who wrote the music for *Flashdance*.)

✦ WHY SHE MATTERS

In the years following World War II, more and more horrors of the Holocaust came to light, and Riefenstahl's reputation suffered accordingly—even though she denied her work was propaganda. Whatever its aims, Riefenstahl's work has provided future generations a glimpse into one of history's most terrifying regimes. Furthermore, her artistry—in spite of her politics—has won her many fans, including George Lucas, whose final ceremony scene in *Star Wars* bears a strong resemblance to similar scenes in her documentary work.

↯ BEST FEATURE: **Her dedication.**
When interviewers asked Riefenstahl why she co-operated with Nazi forces or whether she thought she was in some way responsible for the murder of innocents, she always maintained her good intentions. "In 1934, people were crazy and there was great enthusiasm for Hitler," she once said. "We had to try and find that with our camera."

↯ HEAT FACTOR: **A beautiful and talented woman is hard to resist—although it's tough for most people to get onboard with someone who got along with Hitler.**

While Riefenstahl's excellent bone structure and iconic blonde bob were easy on the eyes, it's her skill with a camera that really stands out. Propaganda or not, and however unpleasant, her work captured what it must have been like for young Germans during the rise of the Nazis.

QUOTABLES

"Artistically she is a genius, and politically she is a nitwit."

film historian Liam O'Leary

"Few filmmakers understood that this picture was a get-up, a 'beautiful sham,' with which the Nazis and their helper Riefenstahl tried to delude the public."

German author Lütz Kinkel

"That's good, then you will only see what's essential. I would like . . . an artistic document on film."

Adolf Hitler, in response to Riefenstahl's declaration that she had no experience with documentary filmmaking

"Only a naïf or rank opportunist could have so disingenuously separated the medium from its message."

author Debo Felder

SALVADOR DALÍ

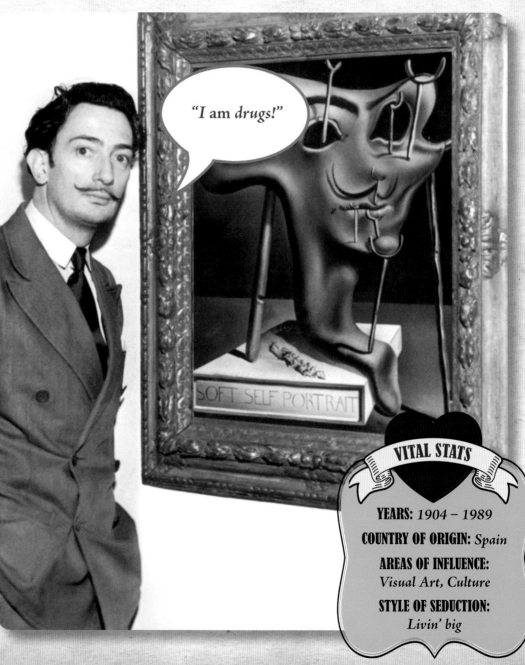

Nº 31

After being expelled from Spain's surrealist collective, Salvador Dalí proclaimed, "I myself am surrealism." He was a very talented, very ambitious, and very egotistical man—and is perhaps the most recognizable surrealist painter to this day.

⇒ DALÍ'S LIFE STORY

Although Dalí's super-straitlaced father discouraged him from pursuing an artistic career, his mother was supportive and nurtured his precocious talents until her premature death when Dalí was still a teenager. Up to that point, Dalí had been attending drawing school in his hometown of Catalonia, Spain, and although he proved very adept in that environment, his creative energies were always looking for new outlets. Or, in his own words, "At seven, I wanted to be Napoléon. My ambition has been growing steadily ever since."

After his mother's death, the young Dalí threw himself into his work at the National School of Fine Art in Madrid. Despite his dedication, he also quickly cemented his status as the resident class clown. He was eventually suspended from the school in 1924 and then arrested on two different occasions for similarly rebellious incidents. Following a one-year suspension, he came back but was then expelled for good.

Dalí didn't let this setback slow him down, however. Never lacking in self-belief, he had his first major (cubist-inspired) solo exhibition in 1925 at Barcelona's Dalmau Gallery, where he met Picasso. A year later, the twenty-two-year-old said "basta" to Spanish life and trekked to Paris. After a brief stint with the Spanish military, Dalí began taking his own theory of aesthetics very seriously (which was unlike him), charting out the origins of a creative framework that would later incorporate science, politics, and philosophy.

In 1930, this purveyor of "hand-painted dream photographs" started hanging with the cool kids —the Surrealists—at an invite-only Parisian gathering. After working with leading Surrealist André Breton, Dalí expanded upon Breton's understanding of objects, viewing them as extensions of the self, rather than something external. And as his creative contribution to this evolving art scene, Dalí eventually offered his "paranoiac-critical" method. He understood the term "paranoia" as the mind's ability to associate two completely unrelated things and then create knowledge from this association (so for instance, you take a clown and then you take a shark and then the mind combines them into a clown-shark—which is terrifying). Dalí put his theory into practice in his paintings as well, which even today seem ripe with both meaning and ambiguity. In 1989, Dalí died of a heart condition at Figueras Hospital in Spain at age eighty-four.

✦ THE STORY OF HIS SEX LIFE

Every great artist needs inspiration at some point or another, and in 1929, the artist took the next step in his career when he met his muse Elena Ivanovna Diakonova—also known, more simply, as "Gala." Gala was the wife of French poet Paul Eluard at the time, but she tossed him aside for the promising surrealist, and they were married in 1934. They remained together until Gala's death, but that's not to say they had an easy or straight-forward marriage. Dalí may not have been too interested in sex, himself, but he was a devoted voyeur. He prompted many liaisons at his home in Port Lligat, Spain, and encouraged his wife to lead a more adventurous life than he himself experienced, but in every other respect, they were a traditional man and wife—they even remarried in a Catholic ceremony in 1958. "But for Gala," he once said, "I would be lying in a gutter some-where covered with lice." Which, when you think about it, actually sounds like the beginnings of a Dalí masterpiece.

✦ WHY HE MATTERS

While his contemporaries were not always impressed with his antics—or with his apparent

---

FOOD AND SEX

Naturally, Dali's theory of sexuality was both fluid and completely bizarre, and because of this, sexual anxiety was one of the features of his paintings most often discussed by art critics. For this surrealist painter, food and sex were completely inextricable. The best encapsulation of this is present in his *Lobster Telephone* in the Tate collection in England. It is, literally, a lobster served on a black rotary telephone. These two objects were used over and over by Dali as tactile representations of all that is carnal.

lobster telephone (reproduction)

---

hostility to "meaning"—Dalí was never bothered by that fact. He held nonsense in very high regard and advocated for an active engagement with the confusion and chaos of the human mind. By sticking to his surrealist guns, he pushed the arts forward into an era of experimentation. His sense of humor pervaded the art world and restored a sense of perspective and even modesty to the of-ten pretentious museum circuit. His body of work so impressed the government of his homeland that in 1982, he received the title *Marqués de Dalí de Púbol*, a signifier of Spanish nobility.

⇒ BEST FEATURE: **His moustache.**

Dalí's thin and severely waxed moustache was voted the most famous moustache of all time by *MSN Him* in 2010. He referred to it as the most serious part of his personality, and it perfectly complemented his precisely plucked eyebrows and perpetually slicked back, shoulder-length hair. As for the less superficial aspects of Dalí's presence, we can't help but admire him for his lifelong commitment to imagination and playfulness in visual art.

⇒ HEAT FACTOR: **Hotter than a lobster telephone (see sidebar)? Is that hot?**

If you're into intellectual weirdos, then Dalí's the man for you. While his arrogance was potentially a turnoff for some, you have to admire his distinct sense of self, as he never seemed to care what anyone else thought. He was undeniably a charismatic character that people couldn't help but be drawn to. This might be a friends-with-benefits situation—soak in the brilliance 'til the narcissism gets overwhelming, then ditch him for someone who likes you for you.

QUOTABLES

"One ought to be able to hold in one's head simultaneously the two facts that Dalí is a good draughtsman and a disgusting human being."

George Orwell

"I have been inclined to regard the Surrealists as complete fools, but that young Spaniard with his candid, fanatical eyes and his undeniable technical mastery, has changed my estimate."

Sigmund Freud

Dalí depicted *"the unreal world with such extreme realism that its truth and validity could no longer be questioned."*

James Thrall Soby

BUGSY SIEGEL

"the man who invented Las Vegas"

VITAL STATS

YEARS: *1906 – 1947*

COUNTRY OF ORIGIN: *USA*

AREA OF INFLUENCE:
Organized Crime

STYLE OF SEDUCTION:
Shootin' straight

N⁰ 32

A slick and fearless criminal pretty much from the time of his adolescence onward, Benjamin "Bugsy" Siegel wreaked havoc from the East Coast to the West over the course of his career. He then invested the funds he earned as a Mafia hit man in Las Vegas.

➔ SIEGEL'S LIFE STORY

Bugsy was born and raised in the Williamsburg neighborhood (now a famous hipster haven) of Brooklyn, New York. His family's poverty seemed to spur his absolutely ruthless pursuit of prestige, success, and power. He started out by extorting money from pushcart vendors (burning down their businesses if they weren't inclined to pay for his otherwise dubious services), and he didn't stop shaking people down and beating people up (and worse) until his dying day. He was indeed a dangerous man to know.

If Bugsy developed a moral code of ethics during his childhood, it certainly wasn't conventional. His Golden Rule had a lot more to do with actual gold than it did with any idea of equality or justice. Known to some for his arresting charm and to others for his apparent indifference toward human suffering, Bugsy used both qualities to his advantage. In his first significant mob partnership, with the similarly notorious Meyer Lansky, he climbed the crime ladder quickly, scaling all

the levels from car theft to bootlegging to gambling schemes. For their bootlegging racket, the "Bugs and Meyer Mob" would steal primarily from rival gangs, eradicating anyone who stood in their way. Bugsy was the muscle (read: trigger finger) behind the operation, and with him on the scene, they quickly cemented themselves as one of the most powerful operations in the New York/New Jersey area.

Siegel and Lansky's operation was eventually subsumed under an even larger criminal network (known simply as the "Syndicate"), with Bugsy assuming a leading role in the "payback" department, aptly dubbed "Murder, Inc." The leading figures of the Syndicate—including Siegel, Lansky, "Lucky" Luciano, Frank Costello, Albert "Mad Hatter" Anastasia, Vito Genovese, and Joe Adonis—bonded, like any gaggle of gangsters, over blood. At Luciano's request, they teamed up for the violent ousting of New York mob boss Joe Masseria in April 1931 and collaborated again in the murder of Salvatore Maranzano in September 1931. Such significant assassinations solidified Luciano's new position as the head of the Mafia in the United States. And with the flourishing work of the headline-ready Murder, Inc., organized crime became an American phenomenon.

⇨ THE STORY OF HIS SEX LIFE

In an uncharacteristically sentimental move, Bugsy proposed to his childhood sweetheart, Esta Krakower in 1929—though it's probably wise to not get too gooey over this fact, as Esta's sister, Whitney, was also a known contract killer. The happy couple had two girls (presumably while they were still a happy couple), Millicent and Barbara, and shared a Waldorf-Astoria Hotel apartment and a Tudor home. Bugsy didn't play by the rules of the law, though, and he treated mo-

nogamy with just about the same level of disdain as he did everything else in his life.

Seductress of mobsters far and wide, the—ahem—full-figured Virginia Hill was a major part of Bugsy's life and may have even played an active role in his death. At age forty-one, Bugsy died a spectacularly cinematic (and somewhat predictable) death when he was gunned down at Miss Hill's Beverly Hills home. She was not present at the time.

⇨ WHY HE MATTERS

While *mobster* and the *Mafia* are household terms today, large-scale organized crime didn't have much of a presence in America before Bugsy arrived on the scene. Once he discovered that he could make a killing by killing, he went at it with the business savvy of a Harvard MBA grad. Although he had a reputation as a savage brute, Siegel managed to sprinkle some glitz on his  profession of thieving and cold-blooded murder, prototyping the image of the glamorous gangster. Case in point: He was never arrested, and he was always dressed to the nines.

Bugsy wove sin and debauchery into America's cultural cloth by turning Las Vegas into a booming, boozy, tourist trap. The Flamingo, a four-floor nightclub built (and soon abandoned) by L.A. business owners, was revived by Siegel's murder money and lavished with the type of amenities the town had never seen before—horse stables, plush carpets, driving ranges, and luxurious rooms. And even though it wasn't able to open with Siegel at the helm, it really did pave the way for the level of excess and spectacle that Las Vegas is known for today. The attention that he garnered from his big city connections brought serious money to Las Vegas—money that the Hollywood set was happy to gamble away. And upon Bugsy's spectacular death, Vegas' reputation for sin was solidified.

⇒ BEST FEATURE: **His swagger.** With a twisted outlook and a crooked smile, Bugsy Siegel made his mark. Even while handling the dirtiest of day jobs, Bugsy always managed to look fresh and clean. In life and in love, the man pulled off dozens of felonies

without leaving a trace. He was good—too good—at being bad. So if he winks at you, run.

⇒ HEAT FACTOR: **Pretty good-looking for a cold-blooded killer.**

1 2 3 4 5

Was he gorgeous? Yes. Was he a good time? Sometimes . . . sure. But was he an absolutely terrifying sociopath? Abso-effing-lutely. With never a hair out of place, Siegel was the epitome of the illicit impresario. He had no qualms about charming your pants off, then putting a hit out on your entire family. Admire him from afar, if you like, but he is not the type you want to bring home for dinner.

QUOTABLES

"He was a frustrated actor and secretly wanted a movie career, but he never quite had nerve enough to ask for a part in one of my pictures."

actor George Raft

"Meyer Lansky and Lucky Luciano helped give organized crime a veneer of respectability; Siegel gave it glamour."

James Toback, writer of the screenplay *Bugsy*

"In a sense he was the Christopher Columbus for the Mob; he went exploring and found the New World in the desert, but Siegel failed to adapt. It is possible that he became confused between the two ways of doing business and thought that because his name was on so many pieces of paper he really owned the Flamingo Hotel. He was wrong."

Wallace Turner, journalist

JOSEPHINE BAKER

"Black Venus"

VITAL STATS

YEARS: *1906 – 1975*
COUNTRY OF ORIGIN: *USA*
AREA OF INFLUENCE: *Dance*
STYLE OF SEDUCTION:
Upstagin' everyone

No 33

Tʜɪs iconic dancer and entertainer left the racism of early twentieth-century America for European fame. Her legacy combines two very different roles: international sex symbol and civil rights leader. Josephine Baker pulled this tricky marriage off flawlessly.

⇨ Bᴀᴋᴇʀ's Lɪғᴇ Sᴛᴏʀʏ

Josephine Baker, born Freda Josephine McDonald, grew up in St. Louis, Missouri, just a few decades after the end of slavery in the United States. She faced extreme racism in her youth, working as a babysitter and housecleaner for wealthy families. At just thirteen, she began touring the United States on the vaudeville circuit, eventually moving to New York City during the Harlem Renaissance and joining the plentiful ranks of African American artists and writers living in the neighborhood at the time. She used her vaudeville training to perform as a chorus girl in some of Harlem's most famous clubs.

Baker went from background dancer to overnight sensation in 1925, when she traveled to Paris as part of a dance venture called *La Revue Negre*. Appearing in little more than a skimpy feather skirt, she capitalized on the French interest in American jazz and the trendy primitivist art movement, whose painters looked to earlier cultures—like those in Africa and Asia—for inspiration. Baker's nearly naked hip-thrusting sent the French into a swoon, and within a year she was starring in her own show at the Folies Bergère, where she sang and danced in a skirt made only of bananas. The French fell in love with Baker, nicknaming her "La Baker." Baker loved France right back; she became a French citizen in 1937. In the following years, Baker began starring in movies and winning the admiration of some of the greatest writers and artists of her time.

the bananas

During World War II, Baker drove an ambulance in North Africa, smuggled secret messages for the French Resistance, served as a sublieutenant in the Women's Auxiliary Air Force, and, of course, entertained the troops. For her service to the French people, she received the Medal of the Resistance and was named a Chevalier of the Legion of Honor.

Despite all she had accomplished, she still faced racism when she traveled back to the States: Clubs denied her service and critics railed against her. In the '50s, she began to campaign for civil rights, arguing publicly with pro-segregation newspaper columnist Walter Winchell and forcing the clubs at which she performed to desegregate. She even marched on Washington with Martin Luther King Jr., wearing her French military uniform.

In another attempt at achieving racial harmony, she adopted a dozen children of different ethnic backgrounds, calling them her "Rainbow Tribe." Unfortunately, her supersized family and some bad financial decisions bankrupted her in 1969. But with a revival show and help from wealthy friends, including Grace Kelly, Princess of Monaco, she was living the high life again in no time. She retired to a castle in pastoral France and died of a brain hemorrhage at age sixty-nine.

✦ THE STORY OF HER SEX LIFE

Baker's love life lived up to her reputation as an international sex symbol. After a starter marriage at the age of fifteen, she married three more times to three different men. According to friend and biographer Jean-Claude Baker, she had plenty of girlfriends, too—relationships she tried hard to keep from the public because of the restrictions and prejudices of the times. The most famous of these was with Mexican artist Frida Kahlo.

BAKERSKIN

Among African American entertainers in the 1930s, skin-lightening concoctions were all the rage. Baker wasn't having it. Instead, she brought a new product to market: Bakerskin, a skin-darkening lotion intended to help Parisian consumers achieve that ideal Josephine Baker skin tone and hue.

✦ WHY SHE MATTERS

Baker's résumé was filled with a ton of firsts: first female African American to star in a major motion picture, first American woman to receive the French Legion of Honor *and* French military honors at her funeral, first woman (that we know of) to wear a banana skirt onstage, and more. Baker was the kind of girl who was always "on," and her divalike antics drew attention throughout her lifetime. Beyond this, the simple fact that she used her body to entertain the masses during a time when people weren't so receptive to dark skin—and prevailed in seducing her audiences—helped to change public opinion about what counts as beautiful. Unlike many of her contemporaries who relegated their acts to black-only performance spaces, Baker demanded that the whole world watch her dance.

↣ BEST FEATURE: **Her chicness.**

In addition to her obvious physical attributes, Baker was seriously glamorous—rocking costumes made of feathers and bananas like they were totally in vogue. Her life offstage was also glamour filled: She had a pet cheetah named Chiquita that she would take for walks around the streets of Paris wearing a diamond collar. Baker had a magical ability to take something totally out of left field, add just the right amount of sophistication, and make it the hottest trend around.

meeeeow!

↣ HEAT FACTOR: **Equal parts seductress and smarty-pants, Josephine Baker had it going on.**

1   2   3   4   5

Baker's phenomenal looks and sexy dances did wonders for African American visibility in the European arena. Even if it weren't for the whole international sex symbol thing, Baker's activism, glamour, and artistic achievement qualify her as a total catch.

QUOTABLES

"The most sensational woman anyone ever saw, or ever will."
Ernest Hemingway

"I wanted to be more like Josephine Baker . . . she seemed like she was just possessed, and it seemed like she just danced from her heart, and everything was so free."
Beyoncé

"Tall, coffee skin, ebony eyes, legs of paradise, a smile to end all smiles."
Pablo Picasso

"[The 1926 Follies performance] might very easily be called rotten, but can be sat through, even to twelve-thirty, because of the perfect delight one gets from Josephine Baker. She makes all the nudity and glitter of the rest (even the so well-drilled Tiller Girls) curiously insipid by comparison."
Nancy Cunard, *Vogue*

FRIDA KAHLO

"I paint flowers so they will not die."

VITAL STATS

YEARS: *1907 – 1954*

COUNTRY OF ORIGIN: *Mexico*

AREA OF INFLUENCE:
Visual Arts

STYLE OF SEDUCTION:
Keepin' you guessin'

№ 34

Frida Kahlo was a visual artist with no real affiliations but with an incredible personal and artistic style. Even her eyebrows became icons. Her paintings drew crowds for their shock value and their beauty.

→ KAHLO'S LIFE STORY

Frida Kahlo was born and raised with her three sisters in Mexico in the early twentieth century. Her photographer father encouraged her to play rough-and-tumble sports like soccer and wrestling. These pastimes were supposed to have aided in her recovery from polio, which she contracted at age six. She walked, then ran with a limp, and continued to exercise and improve until she felt 100 percent. As she grew older, she became more and more fond of her parents' free-spirited attitude, eventually developing a love of dance that seems rooted in her earlier, more active years. Despite her energy and enthusiasm, Kahlo was destined to spend much of her life bedridden. In addition to contracting polio as a child, she sustained a broken spine in a trolley accident as a young adult, and some researchers also believe that she had spina bifida—a birth defect that often results in chronic pain.

It was after the trolley accident, while nearly immobile, that the budding bohemian began to paint. After an agonizing year spent working on a particular self-portrait—a genre that would soon become a favorite—Kahlo completed the disjointed piece and presented it to her then boyfriend, who had been by her side when she experienced the nearly fatal collision. As she continued to paint, her work accrued many layers of symbol-

ism and was frequently accented by images of her Mexican heritage. As means of explanation for her visual inspiration, Kahlo insisted only, "I put on the canvas whatever comes into my mind."

During this prolific period of her young life, she connected with adored muralist Diego Rivera, whom she'd actually met once before while in prep school, and the two fell into a whirlwind romance. She married him in 1929. As their relationship developed, Kahlo's art began to delve into the realm of the surreal, incorporating apparently unrelated objects—though scholars to this day debate whether her pieces can truly be classified as a part of the surrealist movement. Her work also took on a political slant as she became more involved with the Communist Party in Mexico.

Having suffered for years from an extensive list of medical ailments, she died young, at age forty-seven, after having her leg amputated a year prior.

➔ The Story of Her Sex Life

Of all the scholarship dedicated to the life and work of Frida Kahlo, her love life and marriage to Diego Rivera are among the most interesting elements. Kahlo had many lovers in the course of her life, but her relationship with Rivera remains the most famous and, judging by Kahlo's account, the most important as well. Before their official union, Rivera was not just a famed painter but also a famed womanizer, and it seemed he had no inclination to change his ways once he was committed. After their marriage, Kahlo traveled with Rivera as he displayed his murals in galleries and on walls throughout the United States. She finally settled with him in 1933—sort of. They lived in separate but adjacent homes in San Angel, Mexico.

CASA KAHLO   CASA RIVERA

The ultraliberal Kahlo never seemed bothered by the infidelities of her husband and carried on many herself, until his liaison with her sister Cristina drove her to get the classic breakup 'do and cut off her long, luxurious locks. Shortly thereafter, she was devastated by a miscarriage. One self-portrait displayed a version of Kahlo with her hands chopped off and a bleeding heart, indicating her emotional state when she was separated from Rivera, "my child, my lover, my universe." The duo divorced for a year in 1939 while she spent time in Paris but promptly remarried in 1940—though from this point on they spent a lot of time apart, taking lovers of their own. Openly bisexual, Kahlo passed much of her time in intimate relationships with women.

RELATIONSHIP WITH THE TROTSKYS

Kahlo and Rivera's open Communist affiliation frequently got them in trouble, as when the latter painted a giant mural of Lenin in NYC that was soon painted over. After Communist leader Leon Trotsky was exiled from the Soviet Union, he and his wife took refuge in Kahlo's family home, called the Blue House, in 1937. Given Kahlo and Rivera's reputation for extramarital relationships, rumors swirled that Kahlo had had an affair with Trotsky.

➔ Why She Matters

The first woman to sell her work to the Louvre, Kahlo was as unassuming about her art as she was narcissistic about her appearance. Painting simply for the love of the craft, she inspired a legion of creative minds to put a brush to canvas. Hailed by many as a feminist icon, Kahlo made a point not to conform to the aesthetic carved out for attractive women of the time. Instead, she let her Mexican pride guide her to traditional dress and favored ungroomed features. Her eyebrows remain, to this day, a symbol of her pride as well as of her willingness to buck expectations about what she was supposed to be.

⇢ BEST FEATURE: **Her androgyny.**

Her art seems to operate in a strange borderland between reality and fantasy, so it's fitting that Kahlo herself occupied a mysteriously ungendered place in terms of her appearance. She took great pleasure in flowing scarves, embellished jewelry, and impossibly long hair, but she also maintained her light moustache and her signature eyebrows. So what was she? She was Frida. She was as un-pin-down-able as her art.

⇢ HEAT FACTOR: **Look at it this way: She puts a brand upon the brain.**

Kahlo was needy, melodramatic, and reckless with other people's emotions, yet her candor in acknowledging these qualities and allowing those around her to indulge in much of the same cancels out the negative. She played fair. Kahlo was Kahlo, putting it all out there and letting the world observe her agony and her ecstasy. There's magic in those eyes. Dark magic.

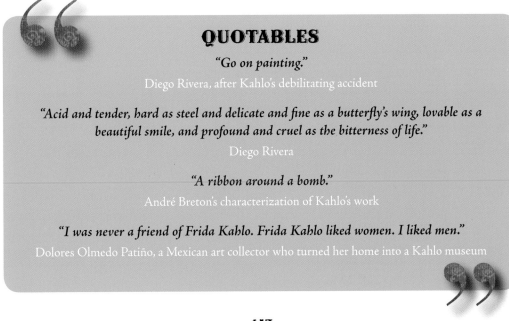

QUOTABLES

"Go on painting."
Diego Rivera, after Kahlo's debilitating accident

"Acid and tender, hard as steel and delicate and fine as a butterfly's wing, lovable as a beautiful smile, and profound and cruel as the bitterness of life."
Diego Rivera

"A ribbon around a bomb."
André Breton's characterization of Kahlo's work

"I was never a friend of Frida Kahlo. Frida Kahlo liked women. I liked men."
Dolores Olmedo Patiño, a Mexican art collector who turned her home into a Kahlo museum

CARMEN MIRANDA

"the Brazilian bombshell"

№ 35

Miranda was at one point the highest-paid actress in America—an impressive feat for an actress who wasn't even American. The actress and singer is credited with helping to popularize Latin dance and culture in the States.

→ MIRANDA'S LIFE STORY

Maria do Carmo Miranda da Cunha was born to working-class, devoutly Catholic parents in Portugal. The family soon emigrated to Rio de Janeiro, where Maria's father took work as a barber and salesman. Following in her father's business-savvy footsteps, Maria eventually got a job in a department store. Belting out Brazilian hits for her coworkers on cigarette breaks, she was overheard one day and offered a gig performing at a nightclub. Her father initially objected to the job, until he learned how much money she could make. Maria took the stage name of Carmen Miranda, using a childhood nickname inspired by Bizet's famous opera, *Carmen*.

By 1928, those nineteen-year-old pipes earned her a recording contract, and just a few years later, she made her first movie, *A Voz do Carnaval*. At the

same time, her album *Prá Você Gostar de Mim* blew up, and she was churning out single after

chart-topping single. Though she spent the decade recording more than three hundred singles and touring South America, it wasn't until 1939 that she got her big international break: one song (sung in Portuguese) in the Broadway musical *The Streets of Paris*.

After Miranda won over NYC audiences on Broadway, Hollywood beckoned the songstress. In 1940, Twentieth Century Fox put her on the silver screen alongside Betty Grable in Grable's first leading role. The studio billed her as the "Brazilian Bombshell," and after signing

fruit hat

an exclusive contract, she began singing, dancing, and acting in films. Miranda came under fire from her Brazilian fans at home for her stereotypical portrayal of a Latin American woman, but the United States' Good Neighbor Policy—a government initiative to advance good relations between

South America and the United States in media and entertainment—kept her on the screen.

But by 1947, when she starred in *Copacabana* with Groucho Marx, Miranda's popularity was on the wane. In an effort to bolster her career, Miranda worked a busy circuit of television variety shows. After one such performance, an exhausted Miranda nearly fainted, collapsing into the host's arms. The bombshell died the next day in Beverly Hills. It is still unknown whether her death was the result of a heart attack or a pregnancy-related illness.

⇢ THE STORY OF HER SEX LIFE

Along with a lengthy list of other lovers, athlete Mário Cunha, businessman Carlos Alberto da Rocha Faria, and musician Aloysio Oliveira were all lucky enough to lay claim to Carmen Miranda's heart during her decades of fame. Yet film producer Dave Sebastian was the only man to achieve husband status, marrying Miranda in 1947. The two separated in 1949, though she never had the heart to divorce him.

⇢ WHY SHE MATTERS

Brazil's first multimedia artist, Carmen Miranda brought a new brand of Latin culture to the international stage, but not everyone was happy about the representation. Initially thrilled with her groundbreaking success as a Latina in the United States, her native country turned against her for playing the role of Brazilian women as brash and sexual character. Despite this controversy, she remains an important figure in the history of Latin American entertainment. Her handprints are even on the Hollywood Walk of Fame.

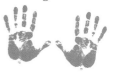

⇢ BEST FEATURE: **Her confidence.**

Singing for white audiences in a language they didn't understand, Carmen Miranda never downplayed her Brazilian culture and femininity, even when scores of women in her homeland began to criticize her persona. Trussed up in belly shirts, stoplight-red lipstick, and piles of gaudy necklaces, she stood solidly on her own two platforms without teetering.

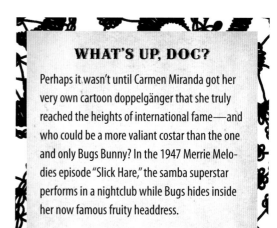

WHAT'S UP, DOC?

Perhaps it wasn't until Carmen Miranda got her very own cartoon doppelgänger that she truly reached the heights of international fame—and who could be a more valiant costar than the one and only Bugs Bunny? In the 1947 Merrie Melodies episode "Slick Hare," the samba superstar performs in a nightclub while Bugs hides inside her now famous fruity headdress.

➤ HEAT FACTOR: **Hotter than Rio during Carnivale.**

1 2 3 4 5

The "lady in the tutti-frutti hat" had manicured, megababe appeal, from her long red talons, to her thin, arched eyebrows, to her wide smile framed by bright lipstick. Whether or not she could carry a tune was a matter of some debate, but she most certainly charmed audiences with her vivacious brand of seduction. She always considered herself "just" an entertainer, not a legitimate actress, but we think she might have been selling herself short.

thin, arched brow

IN HER OWN WORDS

"Look at me and tell me if I don't have Brazil in every curve of my body."

"More affectionate than a kiss is a well-done hug in someone that you love. Have you ever notice how I can give delicious hugs?"

"I've chosen my wedding ring large and heavy to continue forever. But exactly because of that all the time that Dave and I have an argument I feel it like handcuffs, and on anger time I throw it in a basket. Poor Dave, he bought me three wedding rings already!"

ALBERT CAMUS

"Beauty is unbearable."

VITAL STATS

YEARS: *1913 – 1960*

COUNTRY OF ORIGIN:
French Algeria

AREAS OF INFLUENCE:
Literature, Philosophy

STYLE OF SEDUCTION:
Thinkin' deeply

№ 36

Albert Camus was at the center of literary culture in post-war Europe, and he remains a touchstone for college students all over the world. A poignant prose stylist and a deep moral thinker as well, he's the man that every Francophile yearns to be.

⇨ CAMUS'S LIFE STORY

Though he spent most of his adult life in France, Camus was born to poverty-stricken Pied-Noir parents in war-torn French Algeria. (*Pieds-Noirs* was a term given to French citizens inhabiting French Algeria prior to the Algerian liberation.) Young Albert was only a year old when his father was killed at the Battle of the Marne in World War I, and things were not easy on the small family after that.

In his late teens, Camus enrolled in the University of Algiers, and probably endured many an all-nighter as he balanced life as a soccer player and full-time student. Not even a bout of tuberculosis could keep him from graduating with a degree in philosophy in 1936. After graduation, but before the publication of his first novel, Camus wiled the days away in his apartment penning essays on organized rebellion for a number of political papers.

In 1942, while camped in Bordeaux with the staff of French paper *Paris-Soir*, Camus introduced his theory of the absurd with the publication of his essay "The Myth of Sisyphus" and unpacked its meaning in his short novel *The Stranger*. The latter presented an inherently meaningless world in which the characters have to create a meaning of their own. While catastrophic events happen to the main character Meursault, his internal self comes to be satisfied with his own death, regardless of the circumstances surrounding it. The book suggests that life is a never ending but inevitably futile quest to find meaning. Pretty bleak stuff, right? But Camus assures the reader that Sisyphus finds this struggle satisfying in and of itself and urges acceptance of this reality.

Behind the scenes, Camus was working as part of the French Resistance against the Nazis. In 1947, he published his next and arguably most famous novel, *The Plague*, which focused on the same theme of absurdism. It is set against the backdrop of an Algerian town held hostage by disease. Throughout the 1950s, the thinker worked for various human rights campaigns and continued to crusade as an outspoken political activist in the press, winning the Nobel Prize for literature in 1957. At age forty-six, he was killed in a car driven by his publisher.

POLITICALLY INCORRECT

Never one to stray from controversy, Camus joined the French Communist Party in 1935, the same year he received his degree in philosophy. His primary goal in allying himself with the socialism offshoot was to encourage more civil relations between Europeans and Algerians. So it follows that the next year, Camus decided to dedicate his time to Le Parti du Peuple Algérien (Algerian People's Party) rather than the official Algerian Communist collective. This move earned him the boot from the Communist Party; to add insult to injury, he was deemed a Trotskyite, which is the modern-day equivalent of being called a dirty hippie. From that point on, he ran solely in anarchist circles, preaching the gospel of revolution.

✦ THE STORY OF HIS SEX LIFE

Camus's first attempt at marriage came in 1934 with an even greater free spirit than he, Simone Hié, who was a lifelong morphine addict and made a habit of sleeping with the philosopher's philosopher friends. They were divorced in 1940.

Camus was no stranger to adultery himself, having written, "It is an error to make Don Juan an immoralist." Nevertheless, he gave marriage another shot. In a letter to "Yvonne" the night prior to his wedding, Camus wrote, "I'm probably going to waste my life. I mean I am going to marry F." "F" was pianist Francine Faure, whom he did marry in 1940, but it didn't end well. They raised twin girls together, but Francine suffered from severe depression. It is rumored that his indiscretions drove her to throw herself off a balcony in an unsuccessful suicide attempt. Nevertheless, his affairs continued. His relationship with Spanish stage superstar María Casares was sustained for years in cafés and at parties throughout France.

Camus's biographer Olivier Todd said of the thinker's amorous tendencies, "I did not write a book about Albert Camus's love life. Even a telephone directory wouldn't have been long enough for that."

✦ WHY HE MATTERS

Camus offered the international public a means of coping with the trauma of World War II. As "The Myth of Sisyphus" and *The Stranger* began circulating widely and as absurdism (as distinct from existentialism) began to take hold, the hope of finding a sense of internal liberty resonated with despairing readers. Though the origins of his work can be traced to Søren Kierkegaard's influence, Camus is credited with founding and fleshing out absurdism as a proper philosophical theory. The Nobel Committee lauded the thinker's continued refusal to admit to the existence of negativity in his writings: "Inspired by an authentic moral engagement, he devotes himself with all his being to the great fundamental questions of life."

↯ **BEST FEATURE: His fashion sense—oh, and his deep concern for human life.**

The prototype of the collar popper, Camus was never seen without a sleek trench coat, slicked-back hair, and a cigarette dangling from his lips. He was most often photographed with a paramour by his side and an expression of profound apathy on his face. His work belies the don't-give-a-damn image he tried so hard to project. At the heart of each of his publications is a persevering pacifism and a belief that life is worth living—even if it is inherently horrible. Always advocating for an uprising, Camus undeniably had an affinity for drama and revolution, but his real concern for the plight of human beings sets him apart from many artists whose concern ends where their art begins.

↯ **HEAT FACTOR: The flame of his passion never stopped burning.**

We always want what we can't have, and the prospect of actually locking down the elusive Albert Camus is made all the more appealing by his ultimate inaccessibility. Sure, his list of lovers could probably stretch the length of the Champs-Elysées if placed end to end, but he had passion to spare for each one. In his own words, "Why should it be essential to love rarely in order to love much?" Oh, Albert.

IN HIS OWN WORDS

"Man is the only creature who refuses to be what he is."

"Should I kill myself, or have a cup of coffee?"

"Don't walk behind me; I may not lead. Don't walk in front of me; I may not follow. Just walk beside me and be my friend."

EDDIE CHAPMAN

"Agent Zig-Zag"

VITAL STATS

YEARS: *1914 – 1997*

COUNTRY OF ORIGIN: *England*

AREA OF INFLUENCE:
Espionage

STYLE OF SEDUCTION:
Playin' games and takin' names

N⁰ 37

This British double agent had his hands on pretty much all of the information flowing back and forth between Germany and England during World War II—and kept his own life more than a little exciting in the process.

⤳ CHAPMAN'S LIFE STORY

Eddie Chapman was born and raised in Sunderland in North East England. Life certainly wasn't easy, and from a young age he realized that he would have to make his own way in life if he wanted to get anywhere. He enrolled in the British Army's elite Coldstream Guards when he was just a teenager and was in and out of military prison for a variety of offenses before being dismissed entirely. Moving on to bigger and badder things, Chapman began a career in robbery and safe breaking—quickly establishing a name for himself on account of his skills with gelignite. His efforts landed him near the top of the so-called jelly gang and enabled him to hang around in SoHo with the likes of Marlene Dietrich.

The cops were unimpressed, however, and threw the "gelignite artiste" in jail. He escaped to Jersey, one of the Channel Islands off the coast of France, but was soon apprehended again after attempting to rob a nightclub. Chapman, as ever, didn't spend any time dwelling on past mistakes and instead began planning for his future liberation. When

the Nazis invaded the Channel Islands, he offered them his services as a potential saboteur. Impressed by his criminal record (and perhaps by his lack of apparent scruples), the Germans took him up on his offer, and in 1942, "Fritz" parachuted into England on a mission to blow up an aircraft factory. And what exactly does one bring along on a potentially fatal mission like this? A wireless, a pistol, a cyanide suicide pill, and £1,000, of course. Upon landing, however, he pulled a supersmooth move, calling Scotland Yard to propose that he would fake the crime if the Brits let him work for them. They were happy to enlist his services, and thus was "agent Zig-Zag" born.

Meanwhile, the German secret service (the *Abwehr*) were thrilled with the fruits of Fritz's labor. In truth, Chapman and the British had only *staged* the factory explosion, by scattering rubble about the aircraft factory and

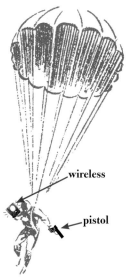

wireless

pistol

ZIG-ZAG

covering the buildings with tarps painted to look from the air like the demolished remains of walls and roofs. With a bevvy of staged photos, as well as a skillfully planted newspaper article in a British newspaper, the Germans were indeed duped. They not only removed their "celebrated agent" to a safe space in German-occupied Norway (where he promptly blew through all his funds in classic playboy style), but they awarded him their highest honor, the Iron Cross. He made his way home in 1944 and, to the dismay of the British authorities, insisted upon telling all in a 1953 book, *The Eddie Chapman Story*. The former spy died of heart failure at age eighty-three in Hertfordshire.

⇥ THE STORY OF HIS SEX LIFE

Like any double agent worth his (double?) salt, Chapman successfully maintained fiancées on both sides of his wartime allegiances. In England, there was Freda Stevenson, who had born him a daughter. And in Norway, there was Norwegian resistance agent Dagmar Lahlum. Both relationships were foiled, though, when the Brits and the Germans sought to use the women to manipulate Chapman and keep him on task. Through it all, though, there was Betty Farmer, whom Chapman had first met in 1939 when she was just eighteen, and eventually married. Zig-Zag remained with her until his death, though his rep as a womanizer

stayed with him. (One bad habit during his time in service involved having affairs with the wives of war notables, then blackmailing them for information.)

HEALTH FARM

A fitting end to the Eddie Chapman story might be a spectacular death on a mission or maybe continued reconnaissance in retirement, right? Instead, Chapman spent his later years running a health farm (basically a spa for clients looking to whip themselves into shape) with his wife, Betty. According to Betty, Eddie constantly bragged about the club, but never participated in any of the fitness classes. How fitting.

⇥ WHY HE MATTERS

The most celebrated British double agent of World War II, Chapman was lauded as "one of the bravest men who served in the last war" by a senior British war officer. Zig-Zag made duping the Nazis look easy. While patriotism couldn't be counted among his strong suits, his information-gathering, seduction, and con-man skills—all vital to life as a spy—were unmatched. He foiled countless game-changing plots, and was so skilled at his trade—and so resourceful—that he served no time in prison for his acts of espionage (although he did serve a variety of sentences related to his safe-breaking hobby).

> **BEST FEATURE: His fearlessness.**

Taking into account Chapman's entire life story, it's evident that this agent had no particular loyalties. So why'd he continually risk his life? His only drive, it seems, was to live life on the edge while looking snazzy with a slim tie, trim moustache, and tall martini glass in hand. He laughed in the face of a potential twenty years in prison, and it paid off, literally. With quick wit as his only true friend, he never stopped too long to consider a task before suiting up to let the adventure begin.

> **HEAT FACTOR: Just about as hot as the information he was smuggling.**

Bad boys always get the blood racing, and this one in particular was a daredevil with money to burn and great stories to tell—especially when the truth didn't suit him! Chapman was handsome, charming, well attired (when he could afford to be), and charismatic. Even the German official whom he deceived for all those years couldn't stay mad at Chapman for long and wound up attending his daughter's wedding. Still, someone who finds it this easy to deceive really shouldn't be trusted. At least, not for long . . .

QUOTABLES

"Don't be silly. Go to bed."
the duty officer in Britain, upon hearing Chapman's story and plea to be a double agent

"In 1944, news trickled through of a mysterious figure in Oslo, speaking bad German in a loud voice, wearing a pepper-and-salt checked suit and given full run of a private yacht. From those details alone, we thought it must be Zig-Zag."
Sir John Masterman, British Intelligence agent

"The women in Chapman's life were attracted to him because of the exact same qualities that made him a superb double agent."
biographer Ben Macintyre

"The story of many a spy is commonplace and drab. The story of Chapman is different. In fiction, it would be rejected as improbable. The subject is a crook, but as a crook [he] is by no means a failure and in his own estimation is something of a prince of the underworld."
an MI5 officer

MAYA DEREN

"the mother of underground film"

VITAL STATS

YEARS: *1917 – 1961*

COUNTRY OF ORIGIN: *Ukraine (then part of the USSR)*

AREA OF INFLUENCE: *Film*

STYLE OF SEDUCTION: *Makin' mov(i)es*

N⁰ 38

Maya Deren was a fearless artist who paved the way for many others not only in experimental film, but also in the larger world of independent cinema. She died fairly young, and as a result, her body of work is small, but her legacy is enormous.

➔ DEREN'S LIFE STORY

Maya Deren was born Eleanora Derenkowsky in the midst of the Russian Revolution. Ukraine was a dangerous place to be a Jew at the time, and at age five, Eleanora moved with her family to America in order to avoid the horrifying pogroms that were being perpetrated. Her father landed a job as a psychiatrist in upstate New York, and a few years later, Deren became a naturalized American citizen—at which point she and her family also adopted the last name "Deren." She was able to spend a few of her teenage years at the League of Nations' International School in Switzerland where she pursued her dream of becoming a writer, but soon after, the budding cinephile returned home to study journalism at Syracuse University.

Her global perspective led Deren to take up socialism while an undergrad student, relinquishing her already loose grasp on her Jewish religion and seeking instead a more all-encompassing solution to the muddled political landscape. Championing a yearning for knowledge, Deren picked up a BA from NYU in 1936, shortly followed by a master's in literature from Smith College.

Maya Deren was never afraid to go with her gut or follow her instincts. In fact, even when doing drudgework for choreographer Katherine Dunham, the wordsmith developed an eye for dancing articulated in an article called "Religious Possession in Dancing." She floated cross-country with Dunham (aka the "Queen Mother of Black Dance") before landing in Los Angeles, where she lived with the well-connected Czech filmmaker Sasha Hammid. Deren created the kind of instant buzz only boozing and schmoozing in the City of Angels can bring, soon cementing her avant-garde filmmaker status with

Meshes of the Afternoon. Made in collaboration with Hammid, the fourteen-minute-long, and seriously trippy, film depicts a macabre dream that dips in and out of reality.

Deren could never get away from the concrete jungle of New York City, as it was rife with material for the expressionistic reflections on identity that she eventually became famous for. She moved back for just a few years before receiving the first-ever Guggenheim Fellowship for filmmaking, which she used to capture her interpretation of Haitian voodoo dance. Although this particular project was never completed, Haitian voodoo was a theme that haunted much of her later work. In 1961, at the young age forty-four, the film provocateur was killed by a massive brain hemorrhage, most likely triggered by her insubstantial diet and longtime dependency on sleeping pills—both common causes of death among the bohemian crowd in the Swinging Sixties.

✦ THE STORY OF HER SEX LIFE

In exploring her sense of identity as an undergraduate student, Deren met and fell in love with Gregory Bardacke, who also happened to be of Russian Jewish descent. After promptly taking their vows, the young couple moved to the Big Apple to put their Trotskyist ideals to the test under the bright lights. While Deren's iconoclastic spirit persevered, her marriage certainly didn't, and the duo officially divorced in 1939.

Their separation paved the way for Deren's more enduring relationship with L.A. filmmaker and photographer Alexander Hackenschmied (later Sasha Hammid). Perched with Hammid in Laurel Canyon, she quickly mastered the tricks of the trade, obsessing over her stimulating projects and her stimulating mentor in equal measure. The two married in 1942.

WHAT'S IN A NAME?

The noun *maya* dates to fourth-century Mesoamerica; it means "measure," with its root *ma* indicating curation or creation. In Sanskrit, the word signifies the power that gives life to static substance, and in Hinduism, maya is an illusion. Maya's adopted first name was thus much more than a name; it was a symbol—an enduring reminder of the fluid divide between tangible reality and the art that represents it.

✦ WHY SHE MATTERS

Though Deren's filmography is relatively meager, it certainly left its mark on the budding experimental film movement. Inspired by her work, Amos Vogel was moved to create Cinema 16 in 1947, a film society in New York City intended to propagate this new wave of filmmaking. Maya Deren has also been cited by some critics as the best representative of postwar independent cinema.

✦ BEST FEATURE: **Her independence.**

Maya Deren was gorgeous in a ghostly sort of way. She broke hearts with her ultrafair skin, wispy arms, and heap of dark curls that always appeared to be in motion even without a breeze. Her pursed and painted lips combined with meticulously plucked eyebrows gave an indication of this sexy artist's almost violent commitment to her work and its principles.

→ HEAT FACTOR: **She blazed trails—and wasn't afraid to scorch a little earth, either—in her pursuit of artistic expression.**

In contrast to the Hollywood icons of the present day, who have a tendency to put their faces on every project regardless of its artistic integrity, Deren remains impressive because she never made herself the focus, even when costs required her to be in her own films. From her inherently hippie nature sprung a humility that allowed her to dedicate all her imaginative energy to her craft without the usual obstacle of one's ego getting in the way. She also lived an amazing lifestyle in Manhattan; the one major drawback being her eventual sleeping pill addiction—but such are the ways of the rich and famous.

IN HER OWN WORDS

"I am not greedy. I do not seek to possess the major portion of your days. I am content if, on those rare occasions whose truth can be stated only by poetry, you will, perhaps, recall an image, even only the aura of my films."

"My reason for creating [films] is almost as if I would dance, except this is a much more marvelous dance. It's because in film, I can make the world dance!"

"When I undertook cinema, I was relieved of the false step of translating images into words, and could work directly so that it was not like discovering a new medium so much as finally coming home into a world whose vocabulary, syntax, grammar, was my mother-tongue; which I understood, and thought in, but, like a mute, had never spoken."

EVA PERÓN

VITAL STATS

YEARS: *circa 1919 – 1952*

COUNTRY OF ORIGIN: *Argentina*

AREA OF INFLUENCE: *Politics*

STYLE OF SEDUCTION:
Smooth operatin'

N⁰ 39

I n Latin American culture, which tended to hold women's bodies in much higher regard than their brains, Eva Perón made history as the first female to effect serious change in Argentinean government. She was also, as it happened, incredibly beautiful.

☞ PERÓN'S LIFE STORY

Born Maria Eva Duarte, Perón grew up in a rural village in Argentina. Driven and beautiful, she moved to the capital, Buenos Aires (the Paris of South America) at just fifteen to become a star. Unlike most other teenage girls with a bus ticket and a dream, Perón succeeded. Before long, she capitalized on her power over her (male) employers and was soon starring in movies and on the radio.

She met Colonel Juan Perón at a party in 1943, and their shared disdain for the ruling powers of the day led to an immediate affinity—if not attraction. They were true partners almost from the get-go, and despite marrying in secret, they couldn't keep their light under a bushel for long and were soon recognizable as Argentina's preeminent power couple. Juan Perón ran for president of Argentina in 1946, and Eva worked tirelessly for his victorious campaign, turning her radio show into an hour-long commercial in Perón's support.

To say she had a knack for propaganda would be an understatement of epic proportions. After Juan was elected, Evita (as she was then known) remained integrally involved in the administration of the country—an unprecedented role for a woman in the conservative South America of the day.

After the election, she made a splash on a good-will tour of Europe, stylishly representing her husband and her country, even meeting with the pope. Despite the glamour that surrounded Perón, her main interests were supporting the poor union workers and the cause of women's rights. Oh, and power. She appointed herself head of her own government-funded foundation, the Maria Eva Duarte de Perón Welfare Foundation, and while spreading the wealth to the country's downtrodden, she simultaneously spread her own fame as the loving and warmhearted mother figure of her country. The press, which was under the Peróns' control, echoed the sentiment, even when the Peróns used less than savory tactics to consolidate their power and "reform" the country's constitution.

Though Evita claimed she was just a humanitarian, by 1952, the Peróns were heading up a media blitz to secure the presidential ticket as

Péron and Péron!

Perón and Perón. The Peróns graciously gave in to their own media pressure and resolved to run together in front of two million people—but they had to change course soon after that. When Evita was just thirty-three, her health rapidly declined. She had advanced cervical cancer but never made this news public, even as she underwent surgery to save her life. When Juan was elected to a second term, Evita was given the official state title of "spiritual leader of the nation." Her health declined very rapidly after that, and before the year was out, she passed away. The country essentially shut down to mourn her loss. Days after her funeral, crowds still clogged the streets around the presidential residency for ten blocks in every direction.

→ THE STORY OF HER SEX LIFE

When Eva Perón first moved to Buenos Aires, she had no money, no connections, and very little chance of success. But she was brave, hugely ambitious, and unbothered by the occasional setback (or twelve). She also knew how to use her looks to her advantage, and although she was able to suppress the details of her rather scandalous background, the basic outline of that shadowy period became visible once she linked up with Juan Perón. People called her a prostitute and a whore,

but while she may have used sex to get ahead in life, it appears unlikely that she ever walked the streets. Instead, she allied herself with a series of the men she needed to know to get work, gain some level of fame, and earn a handsome living. In a life that began with little to no hope, she found a way.

Publicly, Juan and Evita's marriage was filled with intrigue, yet in the bedroom it appears that things were pretty vanilla (perhaps because they both had other interests and priorities). Evita's personal politics, rather than her personal life, remained liberal, as she attempted to legalize the red light district in one important phase of her government career.

→ WHY SHE MATTERS

In 1947, Evita presented congress with a women's suffrage bill. In September of the same year, women in Argentina gained the legal right to vote, in large part due to her careful negotiating. Tirelessly dedicated to first securing a place in the political fabric of the country (even at some unavoidable personal cost), then committed to using this power for at least some good (despite allegations of misappropriation of funds for her own personal gain and the persecution of her political foes as well), Evita was a powerhouse. Infuriated by her country's disregard for the underprivileged, she worked to root out social and economic inequality, at the same time setting a precedent for strong, opinionated women in Latin American culture.

→ **BEST FEATURE: Her sophistication.**
Evita had movie-star good looks and cutting-edge style. Glossy gold curls, red lips, and a neck dripping with diamonds cemented her as an urbane icon—a girl who'd been around the block a time or two, acquired a certain skill set along the way, and then used said skill set to make a difference in the world (and augment her bank account as well).

→ **HEAT FACTOR: Her beauty was an asset for the many Argentineans who had no political voice prior to her appearance on the scene, but she was also dangerously hot when it came to any political opposition.**

1 2 3 4 5

You can't make great strides in politics without making a few enemies as well. We'll never know the whole truth about Evita (due mainly to Evita's own efforts), but we can recognize her fundamental appeal. She made an entire nation swoon. Sometimes people had no choice (if someone tells you to "swoon or go to jail for life," the choice is pretty obvious), but the emotional outpourings often were entirely real. She was beautiful and charismatic; in politics as in life, if she wanted something, she got it. Her sex appeal transcended sexuality and became a political force capable of changing a nation. She was at the center of everything, and everyone wanted a piece of her—but she wanted a piece of everything, too. In conclusion: Buyer beware.

QUOTABLES

"Many people see Eva Perón as either a saint or the incarnation of Satan. That means I can definitely identify with her."
Madonna, when cast as the lead in the film version of the musical *Evita*

"Evitas are raining down on us: saint, martyr, socialist, feminist, fashion plate, fascist, adventuress, whore, witch, wandering corpse."
New York Times journalist Kate Jennings

"She established once and for all that the best political power base resides with the working people. Today, all of our politicians want to be perceived as populists. This was not always the case. Before Evita, those with political ambition courted the elite of the military and the entrenched bureaucrats."
Maria Lagorio, public information specialist for the Argentine Embassy

HELEN GURLEY BROWN

"the single girl"

VITAL STATS

YEARS: *1922 – 2012*

COUNTRY OF ORIGIN: *USA*

AREA OF INFLUENCE: *Culture*

STYLE OF SEDUCTION:
Pinchin' your butt and kickin' your ass

No. 40

Helen Gurley Brown's book *Sex and the Single Girl* offered a radically fresh voice (and perspective) for women in 1960s America. As editor-in-chief of *Cosmopolitan* for more than thirty years, she also forced people to recognize that sex was as important for women as it was for men.

↯ BROWN'S LIFE STORY

Helen Gurley Brown was raised in the Ozarks, in the town of Green Forest, Arkansas. It wasn't a very promising existence—she described it as "ordinary, hillbilly, and poor." Her parents were both teachers, but Cleo, her mother, sacrificed her career to raise Helen and her sister after they were born. When her father got involved in state politics, the family of four relocated to the big city of Little Rock, but catastrophe struck when Brown was ten years old: Her father was killed in a freak elevator accident.

Five years later, the now broke trio moved to Los Angeles, and amid the City of Angels, Brown was, if anything, more pessimistic than ever before. She felt dowdy and was frustrated by her seemingly incurable acne. Brown's self-esteem further plummeted when she realized she would probably have to marry rich to escape her unlucky circumstances. That got her thinking, though, about what other options she might possibly have as a "mouseburger" (a term she coined to describe not particularly moneyed, not particularly eligible young women like herself).

Brown was determined to attend Woodbury Business School in California, after which she entered the *Mad Men*–era world of advertising as a secretary. Shameless about using her feminine wiles to move up the ladder, she seemed happy to exchange favors for presents and promotions from the higher-ups. (Ladies, this was pre-feminism—don't try it at home.) She was later quoted as saying, "My success was not based so much on any great intelligence but on great common sense." Her willingness to promote her sexuality shouldn't take away from what was still a startling and impressive rise from the typing pool to a full-time position as a salaried copywriter.

After gaining insight into the gender politics from stints at nearly every top ad agency, Brown compiled her thoughts in *Sex and the Single Girl*, a treatise on women's sexual freedom published when she was forty. Though the book received mixed reviews, it still sold two million copies within three weeks. Brown's upfront approach caught the attention of Hearst Magazines, which at the time was looking to reinvigorate the struggling *Cosmopolitan*. After being hired as the new editor-in-chief, she didn't take long to make a big impression. Maintaining the overall focus of the magazine (on how to find a husband and keep him happy), she replaced fuddy-duddy housekeeping tips and kitchenware ads with smokin'-hot cover girls (and the toe-curling "keep him happy in bed" articles we know today). This voluptuous visual became the enduring image of the "Cosmo girl"—the well-read but lively young woman who had it all. This wasn't every liberated woman's cup of tea, but under Brown's reign, the monthly sales figures rose every year for nearly two decades.

Brown passed the torch to Bonnie Fuller, original editor of the first U.S. edition of *Marie Claire*, in 1997. However, never slowing down for an instant, Brown stayed on staff as the international editor of *Cosmo* and moved on to large-scale projects like founding the David and Helen Gurley Brown Institute for Media Innovation. In their later years, the couple donated millions of dollars to journalistic and academic institutions.

⤳ THE STORY OF HER SEX LIFE

In 1959, Helen wed the wealthy David Brown, who had previously worked at *Cosmopolitan* and, finding it a dead end, went on to produce such blockbusters as *Jaws* and *Driving Miss Daisy*. Their marriage lasted until David's death in 2010. He was the person who initially encouraged her to write *Sex and the Single Girl*. The book came out just three years after their wedding and spilled all of Helen's scandalous stories from her bachelorette days in such detail that would put the Kardashian sisters to shame.
Well, almost.

Before Helen met David, her MO was to lean heavily on her fresh-faced good looks in pursuit of success or at least some other kind of compensation. After meeting David, she toned things down a bit but set off to preach the good word to a new generation of unwed women, advising them on "how to look their best, have delicious affairs, and ultimately bag a man for keeps," according to her obituary in the *New York Times*. Her message to *Cosmo* readers was all about shamelessness, even when taken to the extreme. Brown never had children and advised her readers to do the same, asserting that pregnancy is fattening and child rearing is menial labor.

⤳ WHY SHE MATTERS

Whereas first-wave feminism focused on equal

legal rights (thank you kindly, Susan B. Anthony), Brown helped to launch a badly needed conversation about real-world rights like birth control and the gender pay gap. *Sex and the City*'s Carrie Bradshaw became an unofficial icon of the Helen Gurley Brown mentality—glamorous, outspoken, and financially independent but not afraid to fall in love. Whether you call it "do me feminism" or "stiletto feminism," it is definitely Brown's legacy—and it's still available at newsstands the world over.

→ BEST FEATURE: **Her confidence.**

While the *Cosmo* girl was most often portrayed as a *Baywatch*-style blonde bombshell, Brown herself more closely approximated sexy librarian chic. With her teased chestnut curls and slender frame, she put almost everyone on the back heel. No one was more self-assured, and no one offered a perspective with more panache. Even in her surgically enhanced nineties, she had a way of letting people know that she had their number—and that she'd soon be calling.

→ HEAT FACTOR: **She didn't start the fire. It was always burning. Since the world's been turning.**

Healthy self-esteem, more than good looks, was the key to Brown's attraction. It is possible to be too confident, however, and sometimes her opinions did appear to go a little too far—as, for instance, when she told the world that sexual harassment was just a form of flattery. So yes, she often traded in hyperbole, but it's hard to overstate her impact on American culture. Just remember, if you do begin to fall under her sway, you should take her with a grain of salt.

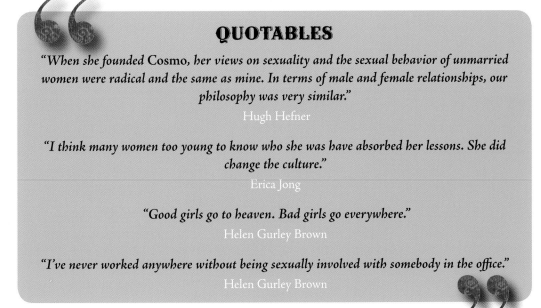

QUOTABLES

"When she founded Cosmo, *her views on sexuality and the sexual behavior of unmarried women were radical and the same as mine. In terms of male and female relationships, our philosophy was very similar."*

Hugh Hefner

"I think many women too young to know who she was have absorbed her lessons. She did change the culture."

Erica Jong

"Good girls go to heaven. Bad girls go everywhere."

Helen Gurley Brown

"I've never worked anywhere without being sexually involved with somebody in the office."

Helen Gurley Brown

FIDEL CASTRO

"El Comandante"

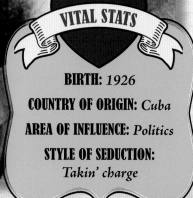

VITAL STATS

BIRTH: *1926*

COUNTRY OF ORIGIN: *Cuba*

AREA OF INFLUENCE: *Politics*

STYLE OF SEDUCTION:
Takin' charge

N⁰ 41

Fidel Castro overthrew the Batista regime in Cuba, making it the first Communist nation in the western hemisphere. On the one hand, he worked to give many disenfranchised Cubans a voice; on the other, Cuba has been accused of many human rights abuses since he rose to power.

→ CASTRO'S LIFE STORY

Castro was born into luxury. His father, a native of Spain, was a sugarcane plantation owner. His mother had been his father's cook and later became his wife. Although Castro's comfortable upbringing didn't quite jibe with his Communist ideology, he was forthcoming about the discrepancy. "It doesn't sound too good to say I am the son of a landowner," he once told an interviewer, "so let us rather say I am the grandson of exploited Galician peasants."

Castro studied law at the University of Havana, graduating in 1950. Eager to start down the path of public service, he worked as a lawyer and joined the Cuban People's Party. He was a shoo-in for a seat in Cuba's House of Representatives when Fulgencio Batista, the former president of Cuba, staged a government takeover, named himself dictator, and canceled the election.

Castro was incensed. After trying and failing to fight the takeover in court, he executed a failed guerilla attack on Batista's army in Santiago de Cuba and landed in prison for two years. Upon his release, he teamed up with fellow Marxist revolutionary Che Guevara to form the 26th of July Movement, so named for the date of Castro's earlier attack. They declared war on Batista's regime, training soldiers in the art of guerrilla warfare to prepare for a coup. After two years of fighting, they succeeded, forcing Batista out on New Year's Day in 1959.

After serving as commander-in-chief of the military, Castro assumed the role of Cuban prime minister in 1959. He initially appeared to be a left-leaning nationalist, but soon began converting private businesses (including American ones) into public agencies and making nice with Soviet Russia. When the United States caught wind of Castro's forays into Communism, they cut ties with Cuba, declaring its leader a dangerous radical. The CIA went so far as to train and fund a paramilitary operation to overthrow Castro's regime. Its attempt to do so, a battle known as the Bay of Pigs Invasion, was decisively thwarted by Castro's forces.

Castro then allowed the Soviet Union to build missiles on Cuban soil in order to defend his nation against another U.S. attack. When a U.S. spy plane captured images of the building sites, the United States squared off against Cuba and the USSR. Known as the Cuban Missile Crisis, the tension-filled standoff became a defining event in the Cold War. It was the closest the world had come to all-out nuclear war at that time.

Meanwhile, Castro grew as a man of contradictions, simultaneously thwarting his opposition at any cost and helping his people by introducing free education and health care—initiatives that won him the presidential election in 1976. His country relied almost entirely on aid from the Soviet Union. When the Soviet Union collapsed, that funding dried up, and Cuba was plunged into economic turmoil. Its people began to depend on tourism and on the money of Cuban exiles who had fled Castro's rule. In 2008, Fidel Castro handed over the presidential reins to his younger brother, Raúl.

✦ THE STORY OF HIS SEX LIFE

Castro was married for seven years to Mirta Diaz-Balart, and the two had a son named (somewhat unsurprisingly) Fidelito. But the couple's domestic bliss was interrupted when Castro's then mistress "accidentally" sent love letters to his wife. The couple eventually divorced.

Castro was reportedly married for a second time to Dalia Soto del Valle, with whom he had five children. He is supposed to have had two other children with two other women, although this number is disputed. Castro likes to keep his private life very private, especially when it comes to his love life, and details are hard to come by.

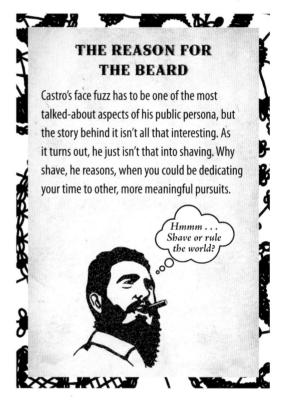

THE REASON FOR THE BEARD

Castro's face fuzz has to be one of the most talked-about aspects of his public persona, but the story behind it isn't all that interesting. As it turns out, he just isn't that into shaving. Why shave, he reasons, when you could be dedicating your time to other, more meaningful pursuits.

Hmmm . . . Shave or rule the world?

✦ WHY HE MATTERS

Castro brought Communism to Cuba and the western hemisphere. At least initially, this move benefited the citizens of his country, who had not been afforded good education or medical care—and who had no political voice at all. Over the course of his decades-long rule, however, many people found cause to complain about the degree to which Castro dominated the political scene and repressed oppositional voices. Castro remains the bogeyman of free market capitalists, Cuban exiles, and CIA agents to this day.

⇒ BEST FEATURE: **Straight talk.**
Castro might keep certain information from the general public, but he has a reputation for real talk in front of a camera. He is up-front with his views, however odious some might find them.

⇒ HEAT FACTOR: **A guy who knows what he wants is totally hot. Unless he wants it all.**

Although Castro's mountain-man beard and trademark cap might get him special privileges in certain hipster bars, it's hard to get over the fact that he was essentially a lifelong ruler. Despots-for-life are great at making whimsical fashion choices and being charismatic, but they are not, as a rule, very good at compromising. Just something to bear in mind if he ever asks you out.

QUOTABLES

"The most honest, courageous politician I have ever met."

Jesse Jackson

"What's amazing here is you've got a country that's suffered an illegal economic blockade by the United States for almost half a century and yet it's been able to give its people the best standard of health care, brilliant education. . . to do this in the teeth of an almost economic war is a tribute to Fidel Castro."

British politician Ken Livingstone

"A revolution is not a bed of roses . . . a revolution is a struggle to the death between the future and the past."

Fidel Castro

"It just happened. There were a whole lot of people in the room. I was talking to them and I turned around and he was standing there."

President Bill Clinton, on shaking hands with Castro

CESAR CHÁVEZ

"If you want to remember me, organize!"

VITAL STATS

YEARS: *1927 – 1993*

COUNTRY OF ORIGIN: *USA*

AREA OF INFLUENCE: *Politics*

STYLE OF SEDUCTION:
Nonviolent negotiatin'

N⁰ 42

As a former migrant worker himself, Cesar Chávez fought hard—and nonviolently—for the rights of migrant workers, helping to create unions on behalf of agricultural laborers in the United States.

→ CHÁVEZ'S LIFE STORY

Chávez, born to Mexican immigrants, grew up on his family's small farm in Yuma, Arizona. When the Great Depression struck, the Chávez family lost their farm and were forced to become migrant workers, toiling in fields and orchards across the West. As a result of his wanderings, Chávez and his four siblings couldn't get much of an education: By his count, he attended sixty-five schools before dropping out without a high school diploma. The family settled in San Jose, California, in the late 1930s. When Chávez's father organized laborers at a local fruit-packing plant, the seeds for his son's future in activism were sown.

When he was seventeen, Chávez joined the U.S. Navy to fight in World War II. Although the period after the war was a time of great prosperity in America, Chávez did not benefit from the economic uptick and resumed his life as a migrant farmer. It was then that Chávez turned to activism, embracing a life of voluntary poverty in order to fight for his fellow workers. At first, he focused on the plight of Mexican-American migrant farmers and joined the Community Service Organization,

helping the exploited communicate with government agencies and become U.S. citizens. Six years later, he split with the CSO to help found the National Farm Workers Association, convincing thousands of workers to demand higher wages.

A turning point for Chávez came in 1965, when the grape growers of Delano, California, cut workers' already low wages. The National Farm Workers Association joined the fight, and Chávez became its leader. He emphasized nonviolent tactics, picketing the fields and enlisting sympathizers for a new boycott. When the grape growers hadn't acceded to the union's demands by the following year, Chávez led hundreds of protesters on a 250-mile protest march to Sacramento to  bring the case before the state government. Then in 1968, Chávez put his life on the line, commencing a twenty-five-day hunger strike in support of a national grape boycott. In 1970, the workers' efforts paid off when the grape growers promised substantial pay raises and signed contracts with the union. Their work had legislative benefits, too: In 1974, the governor of California signed the Agricultural Labor Relations Act into effect, guaranteeing the right for farmworkers to unionize.

After this historic triumph, Chávez continued his fight to improve the lives of workers, focusing on regulating pesticide use and providing acceptable housing for migrants. He died in his sleep at age sixty-six in Arizona.

⤳ THE STORY OF HIS SEX LIFE

Chávez, raised Catholic, married young and stayed married until death did them part. He met Helen Fabela, a high school student, before he went off to war. They wed in 1948 and had eight children together over the next eleven years. Fabela helped her husband with his organizing work, tirelessly supporting his heroic efforts for farmers' rights, while also working to earn money to support their family.

⤳ WHY HE MATTERS

During the civil rights movement, Chávez helped focus energy on Latinos, winning unprecedented rights for workers who had been struggling for survival. Chávez was awarded the Presidential Medal of Freedom after his death.

⤳ BEST FEATURE: **His commitment to the cause.**

Devoted to his cause, his wife, and his moral outlook, Chávez knew more about discipline than most historical leaders. Through setback after setback, he never lost sight of his goal. Even after achieving said goal, he moved right on to another one.

CESAR CHÁVEZ VS. EASTER?

A 2013 Google Doodle of Cesar Chávez made national news, not for its creative stylings but for a controversy surrounding its appropriateness. The problem? The depiction of the labor leader was posted on Easter Sunday—a choice that did not go unacknowledged by Christian groups around the world. While the timing does seem a bit odd, this particular Easter Sunday happened also to fall on what would have been Chávez's birthday. What originated as a simple questioning of Google's motives to celebrate the activist rather than the holiday soon grew into a full-fledged political controversy. Because President Barack Obama had declared March 31 Cesar Chávez Day the previous year, suspicions that this was a religious attack carefully plotted by the White House began to circulate. The backlash was met by a simple response from Google that though it often celebrates the holidays with Google Doodles, sometimes it just wants to switch it up and feature a historical person or event never highlighted before.

 HEAT FACTOR: **Nothing's sexier than a guy who will fight—fairly and squarely—on behalf of other people, for a cause that he believes in.**

1 2 3 4 5

With his thick head of dark hair, disarmingly crooked smile, and tireless passion for advocacy, Cesar Chávez was handsome both inside and out. Whether he was running, marching, picketing, or starving himself for change, he always put the needs of others before himself—and that's pretty sexy.

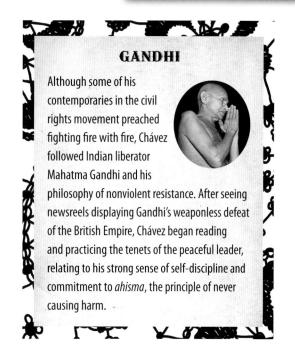

GANDHI

Although some of his contemporaries in the civil rights movement preached fighting fire with fire, Chávez followed Indian liberator Mahatma Gandhi and his philosophy of nonviolent resistance. After seeing newsreels displaying Gandhi's weaponless defeat of the British Empire, Chávez began reading and practicing the tenets of the peaceful leader, relating to his strong sense of self-discipline and commitment to *ahisma*, the principle of never causing harm.

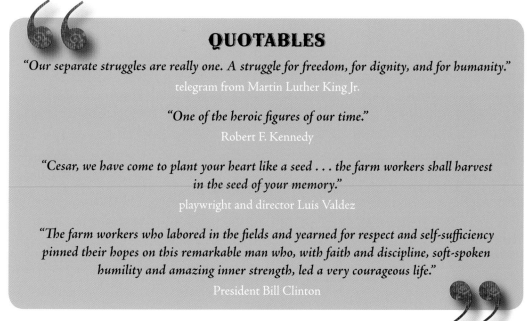

QUOTABLES

"Our separate struggles are really one. A struggle for freedom, for dignity, and for humanity."
telegram from Martin Luther King Jr.

"One of the heroic figures of our time."
Robert F. Kennedy

"Cesar, we have come to plant your heart like a seed . . . the farm workers shall harvest in the seed of your memory."
playwright and director Luis Valdez

"The farm workers who labored in the fields and yearned for respect and self-sufficiency pinned their hopes on this remarkable man who, with faith and discipline, soft-spoken humility and amazing inner strength, led a very courageous life."
President Bill Clinton

CHE GUEVARA

"Saint Ernesto" aka "The Butcher of La Cabaña"

VITAL STATS

YEARS: *1928 – 1967*

COUNTRY OF ORIGIN: *Argentina*

AREA OF INFLUENCE: *Politics*

STYLE OF SEDUCTION: *Bein' radical*

N⁰ 43

Ernesto "Che" Guevara was and remains an icon of idealism and revolt. His involvement in complex, violent struggles resulted in a legacy that is equal parts admired and reviled, but he effected real change around the globe and inspired many people to fight for political improvement.

→ GUEVARA'S LIFE STORY

Che Guevara was born Ernesto Guevara de la Serna to a middle-class Spanish-Irish family on an Argentinean plantation. Although Guevara had asthma, he was a fine athlete and an even better student, graduating from medical school in 1953. The young Marxist's plans about living a comfortable life as a doctor were derailed after he took a motorcycle trip through Latin America and saw the heartbreaking poverty of the people around him.

Guevara wanted to help his people, and he wanted revolution. He moved to Guatemala, where a progressive regime had taken hold. When the CIA funded a coup that overthrew the regime, Guevara moved to Mexico, where he met Fidel Castro. The future leader of Cuba was preparing to overthrow dictator Fulgencio Batista, and Guevara decided to join him. In the Cuban prov-

Fidel and Che

ince of Oriente in 1956, Guevara suffered a defeat by Batista's forces. He then decided to build and lead a guerilla army that aided in the success of Cuba's Communist revolution. When the insurgents formed a new Marxist government, Guevara became a Cuban citizen. As an official representative of the country, he could speak out against the United States' imperialist foreign policy. Through the mid-1960s, he served in various high-ranking positions in the Cuban government: president of the National Bank of Cuba, chief of the Industrial Department of the National Institute of Agrarian Reform, and minister of industry.

Then, suddenly, Guevara fell off the grid. It wasn't until years later that he was discovered to have run off to the Congo to rally a guerilla army. He then moved to Bolivia to create a guerilla group there. Around this time, he wrote his famous Marxist treatise "Message to the Tricontinental," which criticized both the United States and the Soviet Union. He was captured in 1967 by the Bolivian government after a failed insurrection and executed.

✦ THE STORY OF HIS SEX LIFE

Guevara met his first wife, Hilda Gadea, near the end of his motorcycle tour of Latin America. He was a young, arrogant idealist and she, a Peruvian political exile in Guatemala. They fell in love and had a child, Hildita, with whom Hilda stayed behind while Guevara fought in Cuba. When she followed him there after the rebels defeated Batista, he asked her for a divorce.

Guevara married Aleida March just a few days after the divorce was final. He had met her in the urban underground movement in Cuba. They had four children together and remained married until his execution.

✦ WHY HE MATTERS

 Che Guevara was an integral figure in the Communist overthrow of Cuba. His writing and speeches have continued to inspire those around the world who seek an end to oppression through revolt. The ubiquitous photo of his handsome, determined face, reproduced on countless T-shirts and dorm room posters, serves as a perennial reminder of Guevara's unrelenting belief in revolution.

✦ BEST FEATURE: **His bravery.**

The majority of trained doctors don't form guerilla armies and overthrow dictatorships, but Guevara's strong belief in liberating the op-pressed drove him to do just that, even when those efforts seemed hopeless. His irresistible mix of intelligence and action qualify Guevara as a real warrior-poet.

CHE ON FILM

In 2008, IFC Films released the $58 million film *Che,* intended to capture the spirit of Che Guevara's brief and tumultuous life. The biopic was shot in two parts, with the earlier segment covering, via flashback, the jubilant stirrings of revolution with Fidel Castro in 1957. The later segment depicts Che's less-successful revolution in Bolivia and the slow decline that led to the protagonist's death.

When the film was first screened at the Cannes Film Festival in France, the lead actor, Benicio Del Toro, was awarded best actor. Clocking in at a whopping four and a half hours, the film, directed by Steven Soderbergh (of *Ocean's Eleven* fame), appealed primarily to the viewer's sensory reaction and gave only a cursory look inside the mind of the subject himself. Perhaps it's because of this difficult balance that Soderbergh admitted in a later interview that he regrets making the film in the first place. (It's hard to get inside the mind of a global icon, I guess.)

↯ HEAT FACTOR: **Ambition, bravery, and great hair—what's not to love? (Oh yeah, right, that whole death-wish thing.)**

1 2 3 4 5

It's hard to resist an intellectual on a motorcycle who died fighting for his cause, and Guevara's incredible popularity to this day (on T-shirts, in film, on canvas, on posters) certainly has a lot to do with his otherworldly attractiveness—lest that be forgotten. Still, as with anyone who spent his life fighting for change in the world, he played a pretty immediate role in ending people's lives as well as working on other people's behalf. He wasn't just a good guy; he was a complicated man, working in troubled places and fighting for a new start.

warrior-poet eyes

WHAT HAPPENED TO HIS BODY AFTER HE DIED

Guevara's capture and execution were highly anticipated by his enemies. As a result, his captors ransacked his corpse and his meager belongings. They lopped off his hands, preserving them in formaldehyde to prove to Fidel Castro that Guevara was truly the one they had killed. They also divided up his pipe, tobacco, and watch. Forty years after his death, a CIA operative who hacked off a lock of his hair sold it at auction for $100,000.

$100,000

QUOTABLES

"Sometimes people know what he stands for, sometimes not. Mostly I think [the iconic photo of Che] is used well, as a symbol for resistance, against repression."
daughter Aleida Guevara

". . . not only an intellectual but also the most complete human being of our age."
philosopher Jean-Paul Sartre

"Che seemed to be a man who sought death."
Fidel Castro

SYLVIA PLATH

VITAL STATS

YEARS: *1932 – 1963*

COUNTRY OF ORIGIN: *USA*

AREA OF INFLUENCE: *Literature*

STYLE OF SEDUCTION: *Hittin' you in the gut*

№ 44

Sylvia Plath was a midcentury poet whose confessional writing style exposed a roiling internal world. Her work continues to inspire writers and spark rebellious thoughts in readers all over the world.

➢ PLATH'S LIFE STORY

Reading just a few lines of Sylvia Plath's poetry will tip you off that her early family life was a bit rocky. Her parents were both academics; her father, Otto, was a German professor and entomologist, and her mother, Aurelia, had a master's degree in teaching. Otto had been Aurelia's professor and was two decades older than his wife. An extremely strict disciplinarian to young Sylvia, he died of diabetes complications when she was only eight. Sylvia's issues with her father would impact her for the rest of her life, inspiring some of her most memorable poetry but also purportedly hurting her marriage. The same year her father died, her poem "Point Shirley" about the landscapes of Winthrop, Massachusetts, was published in the *Boston Herald*'s children's section. She kept a journal of her feelings since the age of eleven and was published in the *Christian Science Monitor* just after finishing high school.

Heading to the prestigious Smith College on scholarship, Plath carved a place for herself, finally, among other writers and intellectuals. She performed so well that she was chosen for the College Board of *Mademoiselle* magazine in 1953. But this success was cut short by a bout of crushing depression, perhaps triggered by her dissatisfaction with her one-month stint in New York at *Mademoiselle* or due to her rejection by Harvard's summer writing seminar, which she expected to attend. During this depression, Plath's mother recommended electroconvulsive shock therapy, a common treatment for mental illness at the time. It was unsuccessful, however, and Plath attempted suicide for the first time, overdosing on sleeping pills in the crawl space of her house. The attempt was unsuccessful, but she missed a semester of school as a result. When she returned to Smith, it was with an elevated profile and an air of intrigue.

After graduating from Smith, Plath moved to Cambridge on a Fulbright fellowship and, in 1956, wed Cambridge colleague Ted Hughes. Plath and Hughes settled in Boston, and she taught English at Smith, which allowed him to focus full time on his professional writing career.

Hughes's efforts paid off when he won a major poetry prize a few years later. Not long after, Plath gave birth to her daughter, Frieda, and shortly after experienced success with her collection of poetry titled *Colossus*. Sadly, after this point, Plath's most accomplished work was often tied to or prompted by heartbreaking anxiety and depression. Her marriage to Hughes became unstable and was tarnished by his infidelity. During this period, Plath composed several furious poems rife with misandry, including the infamous "Daddy." As her work grew more intense, it became harder for her to find a publisher. As one editor put it, "We didn't feel you had managed to use your materials successfully."

Plath gave birth to her second child, Nicholas, in 1962, the same year that Hughes left her for Assia Gutmann Wevill. The aftermath of the breakup is chronicled in Plath's most notorious poetry collection, *Ariel*. In an attempt to start over, she moved with her two toddlers to a new flat in London. But a fresh start proved to be too little too late: Just a couple of weeks after the UK publication of her novel *The Bell Jar* (under the elegant pseudonym Victoria Lucas), Sylvia Plath committed suicide via carbon monoxide poisoning. She was thirty years old.

✦ THE STORY OF HER SEX LIFE

Plath's feminist view of sex was radical for her time. She was fiercely protective of her right to be just as sexual as her male counterparts, and Ted Hughes was one of the few men she en-

countered who shared her liberal viewpoint. She was captivated by him. Contemporary author Erica Jong writes of their relationship, "Star-crossed lovers always fascinate, and Sylvia Plath and Ted Hughes were surely star-crossed. Their attraction was fierce and they both chronicled it with brilliance."

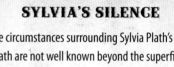

SYLVIA'S SILENCE

The circumstances surrounding Sylvia Plath's death are not well known beyond the superficial details. This is due in part to the fact that few obituaries were published in honor of the celebrated writer at the time of her passing—perhaps because the public did not really want to read about her suicide. It was a truly sad end. One obituary, in the *Wellesley Townsman*, outright lied, stating that she had passed away from viral pneumonia.

✦ WHY SHE MATTERS

Sylvia Plath typified the confessional poetry movement begun in the 1950s. Plath, along with contemporaries like Anne Sexton and Robert Lowell, busted through the *Leave It to Beaver*–style pretense of the decade and shone an artistic spotlight on topics like depression and sexual trauma. "Plath wrote specifically about suicide—her own suicide, much-meditated and plotted—and her much-publicized ill treatment at the hands of her husband Ted Hughes made her into a feminist martyr of a kind," said fellow writer Joyce Carol Oates. Plath was the first poet to be awarded a Pulitzer Prize posthumously (for *The Collected Poems*, compiled by Hughes).

⟿ BEST FEATURES: **A smile to match her sparkling intellect.**

Despite her often-debilitating depression, there are few photos of Sylvia Plath where she's not wearing a glowing, girl-next-door smile. She rocked the Zooey Deschanel bangs way before Zooey was even born. And yet, under her beautiful exterior lay a dark and deeply troubled soul.

⟿ HEAT FACTOR: **Whether you met her in person or only knew her through her poetry, Plath's touch was searing.**

Plath was very photogenic. Very. When you look at the photos, it's easy to forget how difficult her life was, but when you need a reminder, it's wise to go back to her work. Be careful, though, the morbid, teasing, furious passion of her words still has a visceral power. One way or another, she's hard to resist. So give in for a moment, but remember to take a step back when the pull is too strong. Hers is a dark seduction.

IN HER OWN WORDS

"And by the way, everything in life is writable about if you have the outgoing guts to do it, and the imagination to improvise. The worst enemy to creativity is self-doubt."

"Kiss me, and you will see how important I am."

"Perhaps when we find ourselves wanting everything, it is because we are dangerously close to wanting nothing."

"Is there no way out of the mind?"

GLORIA STEINEM

"Some of us are becoming the men we wanted to marry."

45

The 1970s were a time of great advances in the American feminist movement. Gloria Steinem became one of its most visible practitioners when she cofounded the pioneering magazine *Ms.* in 1971. To this day, she continues to be a prominent feminist journalist and activist.

→ STEINEM'S LIFE STORY

Gloria Steinem grew up in Ohio, frequently changing schools and moving to new towns along with her family. When it was time for her to go to college, she chose Smith, perhaps because the Massachusetts campus was far away from her father, a traveling salesman, and her mentally ill mother, whom she had taken care of for years.

After graduating magna cum laude and studying in India, Steinem moved to New York to pursue a career in journalism. Accepting a fateful assignment for *Show* magazine, she went undercover as a Playboy Bunny at the popular Playboy Club in New York and wrote a feature story about her experiences. What started as an interesting idea quickly turned into a hard-hitting exposé that revealed how badly the Bunnies were treated. Sure, the costumes were incredibly uncomfortable, and, yes, the girls were paid substantially less than the company advertised, but the most horrifying, albeit not entirely surprising, discovery was that the Bunnies were treated as sex objects plain and simple.

Although the story was a hit, Steinem suffered for it. It was difficult enough for female investigative journalists to be taken seriously, but Steinem learned this the hard way. She pinned on a bunny tail, and it took quite some time before she was taken seriously again. For roughly a decade after the article was published, Steinem struggled to find work. In 1968, however, Steinem took matters into her own hands and helped found *New York* magazine.

While the Bunny ordeal made her examine the gender politics of her day, Steinem didn't become active as a feminist until the following year. At a town hall meeting, she witnessed both men and women talking seriously about reproductive rights—a topic that at the time was considered to be exclusively a "women's issue." She cemented her role as a leading feminist  and public figure when, in 1971, she founded *Ms.* with the mission of creating a place where women could read and write about important issues without the pressure of male oversight. This groundbreaking move instantly made Steinem an important public figure and a highly coveted speaker. She soon established a rep as a public intellectual embroiled in the fight for the right of women to speak their minds without fear of punishment.

Steinem helped organize a number of activist groups, including the Coalition of Labor Union Women, Women's Action Alliance, and the National Women's Political Caucus. She also helped found the Ms. Foundation for Women, with the goal of providing resources for all women who wanted equal rights. In 2005, she helped start the Women's Media Center, which aims to help women become a more visible and powerful force in the media. In addition to her journalistic writing, Steinem has written many books and essays about feminism and self-esteem.

→ THE STORY OF HER SEX LIFE

Steinem got pregnant after college but had no desire to become a housewife. She has spoken very publicly about her decision to have an abortion. She once said, "A liberated woman is one who has sex before marriage and a job after." According to this definition, she was definitely liberated. After gaining notoriety and fame (through her work, it should be noted) she was involved with several celebrity boyfriends, including TV producer Mike Nichols and real-estate billionaire

Mort Zuckerman. Steinem's first and only marriage occurred at the age of sixty-six, when she wed David Bale (Christian Bale's father), purportedly because he needed a green card.

CIA CONNECTION

While in India after college, Steinem was approached by a CIA agent to oversee a front called the Independent Service for Information. In that role, Steinem accepted money from the CIA to spy on Communist student groups. Her involvement wasn't revealed until decades later, and her reputation was damaged by working for the shadowy government agency during the Vietnam War. Steinem, for her part, has defended the CIA as "liberal" and "nonviolent."

→ WHY SHE MATTERS

There were certainly other feminist magazines before Ms., but Steinem's publication was the first with mass appeal. Steinem made feminism accessible—even trendy—for women nationwide. The success of Ms. paved the way for magazines like Bust and Rookie and blogs like Jezebel and XOJane. Part of Steinem's enduring appeal was a trait that set her apart from her contemporaries: her pro-sex message—one that didn't exclude women who wanted to maintain a traditionally feminine appearance.

❧ BEST FEATURE: **Her outspoken nature.**

In 1970s feminist circles, Steinem's trendy aviator sunglasses and long hair—  sometimes blonde, sometimes brunette, often highlighted—set her apart from those feminists who believed that looking good discredited their message. Equally sexy: Steinem's populism. She spoke out in favor of any woman who felt oppressed by living in a man's world, whether or not she wore lipstick.

❧ HEAT FACTOR: **Hot enough to make the 1970s seem cool again.**

Even if it weren't for her tireless advocacy for women's equality, Steinem would still be crushable. She became the public face for second-wave feminism for a reason: She's bold and brave and spoiling for a fight. And lucky for her, the culture wars have provided her with a steady stream of battles.

QUOTABLES

"Materialism has defeated feminism as well. In a sign of the times, Gloria Steinem was on the picket line when the first American De Beers store opened on Fifth Avenue in June 2005, protesting the evictions of Bushmen in Botswana to make room for diamond miners and the charges that the company dealt in 'blood diamonds' used to finance civil wars in Africa. Her presence meant nothing to young Hollywood beauties who are pleased to shill for the diamond industry in magazine layouts and personal appearances."

New York Times journalist Maureen Dowd

"She is so deluded that she genuinely believes she speaks for all women. She's a victim of her own success. I liked the early Steinem. There was once a survey conducted for Time about who would make a good candidate for the first female president, and I wrote in Gloria Steinem. But now? Gloria Steinem is dissing men and dissing fashion and she's out having her hair streaked at Kenneth's. She became a socialite with a coterie."

author Camille Paglia

"(Steinem) was my hero. Why do they hate me? I'm a feminist!"

politician Sarah Palin

JANE GOODALL

"the woman who redefined man"

VITAL STATS

BIRTH: 1934

COUNTRY OF ORIGIN: England

AREA OF INFLUENCE:
Ethology

STYLE OF SEDUCTION:
Gettin' in your head

No.
46

W ith more than half a century of research into the lives of chimpanzees under her belt, Jane Goodall has revolutionized the way human beings understand their relationship to animals. Because of her work, we now have a better understanding of both animals and ourselves.

⇢ GOODALL'S LIFE STORY

When she was only a baby, Goodall's father, Mort, presented her with a stuffed chimpanzee named Jubilee. Although her mother's friends found the toy terrifying, she took it with her everywhere—she still has it to this day.

From an early age, Goodall was fascinated by nature, but growing up in London, she didn't have access to many animals besides her toy chimp. Once, out of desperation, she grabbed a bundle of earthworms from her garden and took them to bed with her, only returning them to the dirt after her mother informed her they would die without it. When World War II started, the family moved from London to the south coast of England, where Goodall had more opportunities to observe the natural world.

When Goodall was twenty-two and working as an assistant at a London film studio, her friend, Clo, sent her an invitation to stay at her family's farm in Kenya. Thrilled at the prospect of

such a trip, Goodall moved back to her parents' house and worked as a waitress to save money. Her diligence paid off—after a year, she had the funds to set sail. In 1957, she made the journey to Africa, where her vacation took a serendipitous turn when she met the famous archaeologist and paleontologist Louis Leakey. The elder scientist was impressed with Goodall's passion for animals and recognized her as one of his kind, inviting her on a fossil-hunting trip. Their collaboration went brilliantly, and after a few years, he hired her to lead a study of chimpanzees in Tanzania. It was there that Goodall discovered that chimpanzees use tools—a trait previously thought to be exclusive to humans. Leakey was so impressed that he encouraged Goodall to enroll in the doctoral program at Cambridge University, even  though she hadn't completed her undergraduate studies, going so far as to find the funding for her tuition himself.

After earning her PhD in ethology (the study of animal behavior), Goodall returned to Tanzania and her chimps. Unlike her colleagues, Goodall thought of chimps as individuals with distinct personalities. This perspective informed her impressive research into the inner workings of chimpanzee society, the results of which she published in *National Geographic*. Her article earned her enough attention—and funding—to found a research center.

Goodall continued her chimpanzee research for twenty-five years, then broadened her mission to include not just researching the behavior of chimpanzees, but also protecting the well-being of all animals and the environment. Today she travels the world, speaking out for the conservation of wildlife habitats.

✦ THE STORY OF HER SEX LIFE

Goodall's first husband was dashing Dutch photographer and filmmaker Hugo van Lawick. They met in the jungle when *National Geographic* sent him to photograph Goodall's chimp colony. A year after her article appeared, the two were married. They had one son, Hugo, whom they nicknamed Grub. A decade later, the pair split, and the following year Goodall and Tanzania's national park director Derek Bryceson wed. The couple fought side by side to preserve the African bush until Bryceson's death in 1980. Goodall has not remarried since.

✦ WHY SHE MATTERS

Before Jane Goodall's groundbreaking research, people had a fairly human-centric view of the natural world: Because (the thinking went) animals are wild and mute and people are civilized and hyperlinguistic, we can kill all the animals, or at least mess up their habitats. Then Goodall came along, proving how close we are to our primate cousins and breaking apart a worldview that put humans at the center of everything. Dissatisfied with simply changing the views on chimpanzees, she continues to fight for other endangered species and the environment to this day.

WORLD WAR II

Jane Goodall's work is guided by her strong belief that all creatures should be treated with respect, but the event that introduced her to ethics had little to do with animals. Growing up during World War II, Goodall saw pictures of concentration camp victims in the newspaper. These shocking images hardened her resolve to fight wickedness in the world in whatever way she could.

➔ BEST FEATURE: **Her sympathetic nature.**
When Jane Goodall discussed her research project in Gombe, Tanzania, with her professors at Cambridge, she was told that she'd done everything wrong. But little did they know that by eschewing the rules, Goodall would change animal research forever.

➔ HEAT FACTOR: **She had the ability to charm (and understand) man and ape alike.**

Goodall's romantic life and her professional career are both remarkable in that she had a huge impact despite an apparently casual attitude. She was confident enough to go with the flow but talented enough to unravel a much deeper meaning in the course of her travels.

JANE'S CELEBRITY STATUS

Jane Goodall's fanbase is not without its fair share of celebrities, including Angelina Jolie, Charlize Theron, Pierce Brosnan, and singer-songwriter Dave Matthews of the Dave Matthews Band. These famous fans lent their support to Goodall by starring in or helping promote the documentary Jane's Journey. Matthews, for example, helped organize and performed at several benefits bearing Goodall's name, and ultimately, gave full voice to his do-gooder crush when he sang "Bartender" to her, on film, in a cozy room beside a fireplace.

QUOTABLES

"Now we must redefine 'tool,' redefine 'man,' or accept chimpanzees as humans."
Louis Leakey, on Goodall's discovery of chimps using tools

"Goodall's detailed, engaging descriptions of chimpanzee society transformed our notions of what it means to be a primate—and what it means to be human."
Sierra magazine

"She is one of the most decent people alive today. She is extraordinarily good-natured. The nice thing about her is that we often think about environment, and good will, as this very soft, lovely thing, and she has that, but she's a fighter."
Angelina Jolie

ROBERTO CLEMENTE

"El Primer Latino"

Nº 47

R oberto Clemente was a class act if ever there was one—and a phenomenal baseball player to boot. He was the lynchpin of the Pirates' lineup throughout the 1960s. His dominance only ended (tragically) as a result of a fatal plane crash.

→ CLEMENTE'S LIFE STORY

Roberto Clemente Walker was born in the summer heat of Barrio San Antón, Carolina, Puerto Rico, in 1934. The youngest of seven children, he helped the family make ends meet by carting milk cans to and from a neighbor's house. The money that he was able to save for himself he put toward the purchase of his own bicycle. Clemente was more interested in sports than school (though his mother always dreamed he'd become an engineer) and regularly rode his two-wheeler over to the Sixto Escobar Stadium to watch the games from just outside the fence. His favorite player was the then Negro League star Monte Irvin, who eventually let Clemente carry his glove for him.

As he grew older, Clemente made local headlines not only in baseball but also in track and field. But baseball was always his true passion, and by age sixteen he was playing for the amateur Ferdinand Juncos team. Before he graduated high school, the baseball prodigy was scouted by Al Campanis of the Brooklyn Dodgers and initially offered a $10,000 bonus. Clemente preferred to wait until after graduation to accept, even though the offer kept rising—eventually amounting to more than $30,000. The scout who had spotted him later reported, "Clemente was the greatest natural athlete I have ever seen as an amateur free agent."

After Clemente had a stint in the minor leagues, the Dodgers sent him north to play for the Montreal Royals in the International League in 1954. From Montreal, Clemente was drafted by Pittsburgh (a place he knew very little about) to play for the Pirates. Western Pennsylvania wasn't exactly a racial melting pot, and just as he had in Montreal, Clemente struggled with the language barrier and animosity from players and fans alike. Despite these setbacks, Clemente knocked it out of the park. In the seventeen years he played for the Pirates, he became the first Hispanic player to win a World Series as a starter in 1960 and the first to receive an MVP Award, in 1966. Playing in every All-Star game in the 1960s and receiving a Gold

Glove every season after 1961, Clemente went on to receive a World Series MVP Award in 1971. It doesn't end there—he was the National League batting champion four separate times (1961, 1964, 1965, and 1967), and his best season ended with him sitting on a .357 batting average, with 23 home runs and 110 RBI. So yeah, he could hit a baseball pretty well. He was also an incredible outfielder, winning twelve Gold Gloves over the course of his career.

As if that wasn't enough, Clemente also worked between seasons to provide food and other necessities to impoverished citizens in developing countries. It was on one of his goodwill trips to Nicaragua in 1972 that tragedy struck: The engines of his plane exploded, and the plane crashed into the sea. Clemente's remains were never found.

⇝ THE STORY OF SEX LIFE

Roberto Clemente married Vera Zabala after meeting her in a drugstore in 1963, and the couple had three children together—all of whom were born in Puerto Rico, upon Clemente's insistence. Other than that, there's not much to tell. He was, by all accounts, a great athlete, a great philanthropist, and a dedicated family man. Few people with as much talent as Clemente have lived a life so free of scandals.

⇝ WHY HE MATTERS

The first Latin American to be inducted into the National Baseball Hall of Fame, Roberto

Clemente became a household name due to his uncanny ability both at the plate and in the field. He finished his career with exactly three thousand hits, and, in the words of former catcher Tim McCarver, had a "howitzer" for an arm. In honor of his philanthropic work, Major League Baseball now presents the Roberto Clemente Award to a player whose philanthropy matches the example set by Clemente. As the first Latin American Hall of Famer, Clemente paved the road for future Hispanics to expect success unmarred by prejudice in their baseball careers and gave Latino youth a role model in both athleticism and character.

⇝ BEST FEATURE: **His classiness.**

With fantastic bone structure and biceps set off by his iconic black-and-yellow uniform, Clemente could have been a lady killer, but he chose to be a family man instead. He dressed in a coat and tie when not on the field, exhibiting an unpretentious formality. His easy smile and friendly nature in the locker room were the perfect counterpoint to his grimace at the plate. No matter what the time or where the place, from his youth in Puerto Rico to his charity work as an adult, Roberto Clemente was pure class.

→ HEAT FACTOR: **The question is: Has there ever been a hotter pirate?**

1 2 3 4 5

This Most Valuable Heartthrob puts blood-doping, booze-cruising, cash-squandering, big-budget athletes to shame. Always putting others first, Clemente overcame adversity without breaking a sweat and turned his well-deserved accomplishments in the United States into good fortune for his friends, family, and community in Puerto Rico. Case in point: His first purchase with his Major League salary was a new house for his parents in Carolina.

To: mom and dad

CLEMENTE'S PASSION

Growing up, Roberto Clemente didn't have the resources to play a proper game of baseball—and even if he did, he didn't have friends who could play at anything like his level. No other sport or hobby could occupy his attention, however, so he set to work making a bat out of a guava tree branch and tied a coffee bean sack into a glove. Using similar materials for a ball, he played pickup games with whomever he could wrangle up around the neighborhood. Eventually he did succeed in joining a team, much to his parents' displeasure. The muddy field was littered with rocks and debris from the towering trees, but no obstacle could get in between Clemente and the game he loved. In fact, he became so obsessive that he preferred staying out and catching flies to coming home for dinner, which prompted his mother to attempt to burn his makeshift bat in the stove. Thankfully, Clemente pulled it safely from the flames.

IN HIS OWN WORDS

"I want to be remembered as a ballplayer who gave all I had to give."

"Why does everyone talk about the past? All that counts is tomorrow's game."

"Any time you have an opportunity to make a difference in this world and you don't, then you are wasting your time on Earth."

BRUCE LEE

"the Little Dragon"

VITAL STATS

YEARS: *1940 – 1973*

COUNTRY OF ORIGIN: *USA*

AREAS OF INFLUENCE:
Film, Martial Arts

STYLE OF SEDUCTION:
Movin' fast

№ 48

One of the first Chinese actors to become a bona fide American movie star, Bruce Lee played an important role in making karate and other martial arts a popular American pastime.

→ LEE'S LIFE STORY

Bruce Lee was born in 1940, in San Francisco, with the original name Lee Jun Fan. His family moved to Hong Kong shortly after their energetic fourth son was born, but unfortunately their time in Hong Kong largely coincided with the Japanese occupation, an era of severe poverty and violence.

When the occupation ended, Bruce ran wild in the ravaged streets. But after one brawl too many, his father laid down the law: If his son was going to be a warrior, he was going to do it right. Lee's father started teaching him t'ai chi ch'uan, a martial arts discipline centered on self-defense. His father also happened to be an actor and a comedian in the Cantonese opera, whose connection to the entertainment industry in Hong Kong helped secure numerous film roles for young Bruce (his adopted nickname) before his eighteenth birthday. And with his newfound skills and natural good looks and charm, it didn't take long for fame and fortune to start knocking at the door.

Lee remained a serious and dedicated student and practitioner of martial arts throughout his life, but he never abandoned the spirit of a street-fighting man. This was especially true of him as a youth, and thus, after perhaps one scrap too many, his parents shipped him off to the West Coast. He landed at the University of Washington in Seattle, where he studied drama and met his future wife, Linda. Bruce's dreams went beyond academic achievement, however, and he eventually dropped out of college and moved to California to open a martial arts studio in Oakland.

Lee made the jump from martial arts teacher to martial arts star when he was cast in the *Green Hornet* television show, based on the comic book series. Although the show was canceled after only one season, Lee starred in a

the Hornet's side "kick" Kato

number of popular martial arts movies in Asia. U.S. moviegoers didn't catch on to Lee at first, but Chinese audiences flocked to see him play a cowboy, a secret agent, and, yes, a kung fu master. While wowing global audiences, Lee developed his own martial arts program, Jeet Kune Do—"The Way of the Intercepting Fist." This fighting style relies on a fluid fighting motion and surprise attacks, tenets that Lee outlined in a posthumously published book, *The Tao of Jeet Kune Do*, and which he taught to a coterie of devoted students, including, most notably, Chuck Norris.

Before long, Lee was a global star, and Hollywood couldn't help but catch on. Lee starred in *Enter the Dragon*—his first and only film produced with American audiences in mind—in 1969. More roles were intended to follow, but only months after finishing the film, *Enter the Dragon*, Lee came down with a headache and died from an allergic reaction to his pain medication. He was only thirty-two.

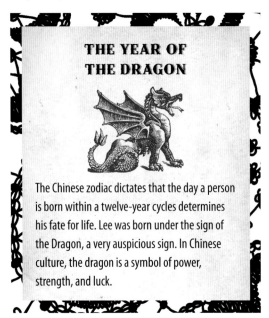

THE YEAR OF THE DRAGON

The Chinese zodiac dictates that the day a person is born within a twelve-year cycles determines his fate for life. Lee was born under the sign of the Dragon, a very auspicious sign. In Chinese culture, the dragon is a symbol of power, strength, and luck.

➤ THE STORY OF HIS SEX LIFE

Although Lee's bare chest was often on display, his love life is enshrouded in rumor and speculation. His parents disapproved of his childhood sweetheart, but *perhaps* coincidentally, she appeared in one of his early films. He shook off the woman his parents attempted to fix him up with when he left China, but nobody knows if that split was intentional. According to his little brother, once Lee moved to the States, he rarely left the house without a girl on each arm. However, one aspect of his romantic history is certain: He married fellow University of Washington classmate Linda Emery, with whom he had two children.

➤ WHY HE MATTERS

Bruce Lee fought tirelessly for the global acceptance of the martial arts—an athletic discipline once thought to be the exclusive domain of Asian cultures. When Lee first caught Hollywood's attention, his roles were limited to parts specifically written for Asians. But Lee knew he was destined for bigger things. Through persistence and sheer force of will, he became one of American cinema's most iconic stars, regardless of race.

➤ BEST FEATURE: **His ferocity.**

Bruce Lee's sex appeal can be easily appreciated by watching the climactic fight scene of *Way of the Dragon*, a clip readily available on YouTube. Watch him unbutton his shirt as he squares off against his opponent, Chuck Norris. Notice his outstanding musculature as he pops his shoulders while touching his toes, and the playful menace of his gaze. But Lee was no mere beefcake—he was a warrior-poet, one who could defeat an opponent with a high kick and then outline the philosophical reasons behind doing so.

→ HEAT FACTOR: **If anything, he burned *too* brightly.**

1 2 3 4 5

Bruce Lee's tireless dedication to his craft is admirable, his balletic fighting style is the envy of every action movie fan, and his good looks were Hollywood ready; but if you're into quiet nights at home, he's probably not your man. If you're into a good time and a good fight, however, look no further.

QUOTABLES

"When Bruce Lee kicked, you don't shut your eyes. Because when you shut your eyes, you cannot see Bruce Lee kick; it's so fast! Human beings cannot move like cartoon, that's the fastest you can be. Even Muhammad Ali or Mike Tyson, their punches are fast, but you still can see [them]."

Jackie Chan

"Bruce Lee had a very—I mean a very—defined physique. He had very little body fat. I mean, he probably had one of the lowest body fat counts of any athlete. And I think that's why he looked so believable."

Arnold Schwarzenegger

"We look at Bruce Lee as a lifestyle."

daughter Shannon Lee

"I liked Bruce's cockiness because he was never cocky in an 'ugly' manner. His cockiness was quite 'cute.'"

close friend Jhoon Rhee

HUEY P. NEWTON

"*You can jail a revolutionary, but you can't jail the revolution.*"

VITAL STATS

YEARS: *1942 – 1989*

COUNTRY OF ORIGIN: *USA*

AREA OF INFLUENCE:
Civil Rights

STYLE OF SEDUCTION:
Bein' real

No 49

The cofounder of the Black Panthers, a group that advocated for African American rights, Huey Newton worked against a system that was stacked against him. But his trouble with the law cast a shadow over his efforts, leaving a legacy clouded by charges of violence but also illuminated by moments of real brilliance.

↝ NEWTON'S LIFE STORY

Huey Percy Newton was born in Louisiana, the last of seven children. His father was a minister, a sharecropper, and a black man in the American South—a tough position to be in at the time. After giving his white bosses a piece of his mind (and nearly being lynched as a result), he took his family west to Oakland, California. Huey's namesake was the former governor of Louisiana who had been more than slightly corrupted by his power, but who had also made a positive impact on the lives of many of Louisiana's citizens. The name didn't do Huey any favors, however. Despite his parents' best intentions, cruel nicknames like "Baby Huey" and taunts like "Huey P. goes wee wee" landed Huey in fight after fight after fight. He got a reputation as a detention junkie and was chucked out of the school system after nearly thirty suspensions—still illiterate but with a diploma in hand. He claimed that when he finally learned to read, the first book he

"Baby Huey"

completed was Plato's discourse on the meaning of justice, *The Republic.*

Newton expanded his education by enrolling in Merritt College in Oakland, studying law at San Francisco Law School, and plunging into the theories of Karl Marx and Malcolm X. The dynamo claimed he initially took a class on criminology to expand his own criminal repertoire and to learn about different types of criminals while figuring out which type of enemy of the state he wanted to be. He and fellow Merritt College student Bobby Seale founded the Black Panthers (then called the Black Panther Party for Self Defense) in 1966 to help ensure that blacks would begin to receive equal rights and equal protection under the law. Serving as the minister of defense of this left-wing organization, Newton committed himself to developing what he called "revolutionary humanism," based on Marxist-Leninist theories. Continuing to educate himself as he pursued his larger cultural goals, Newton got a PhD in social philosophy from UC Santa Cruz. His doctoral thesis was titled *War Against the Panthers: A Study of Repression in America.*

Such was the bias against them, that positive and sustainable Black Panther programs (such as providing free breakfast to children) were often overshadowed in the media by stories related to violence and guns. In 1967, the Black Panthers marched into the California State Assembly bearing arms, causing a media frenzy. Newton was a person of special interest for both local law enforcement and the U.S. government, so perhaps it's not surprising that he faced many criminal charges in the course of his life, but the nature of his alleged crimes remains cause for concern. Newton had a conviction for manslaughter, which was overturned by the California Courts of Appeal, but he later fled the country following a variety of other charges including murder and possession of a handgun. He eventually returned to the United States and served less than a year for the handgun charge. At age forty-seven, he was shot and killed by a member of the Black Guerrilla Family, a ring of drug dealers that operated in the California prison system, in what is rumored but was never proven to be a drug-related incident.

↬ THE STORY OF HIS SEX LIFE

Newton was married to two doting women. His first wife, Gwen Fontaine, sported an Afro that matched his own and handled paperwork and administrative tasks for the Black Panthers. Ever loyal, she stayed by his side through his jail sentences and fled with him to Cuba after he was charged with the murder of seventeen-year-old prostitute Kathleen Smith.

Equally dedicated to the Black Panthers' cause, Fredrika Slaughter met Huey as a youth member of the Black Panthers. The two married in 1981 and remained wed until his death, after which she created a nonprofit foundation in his name. She still serves as the president of the Huey P. Newton Foundation.

↬ WHY HE MATTERS

Raised to resist the status quo and to fight against injustice wherever he saw it, Huey Newton ushered in a new era of African American empowerment with the Black Panthers, encouraging black youth to rise up and demand what was rightfully theirs—and take what was denied them. Even after his passing, the controversy surrounding his legacy continues: Rapper Wiz Khalifa's 2010 song "Huey Newton" was the subject of much debate in 2012 on account of its blithe treatment of Newton's historical legacy. Newton remains an important symbol of the struggle for equality in contemporary America.

↘ BEST FEATURE: **His fearlessness.**

Newton once wrote, "My parents taught me to be unafraid of life and therefore unafraid of death," and his actions show that his life was nothing if not boldly lived. Most often photographed with a giant coif of gorgeous dark hair and sporting a jacket and button-down, he challenged the camera with his defiant gaze. His abuse of drugs and alcohol and his alleged history of violence are certainly strikes against him, but when he was a young idealist, just starting out in life, he was a hard man to say no to.

↘ HEAT FACTOR: **Certainly hotheaded. Often with justification, but sometimes without.**

On the one hand, Huey Newton was handsome, charismatic, and determined to make a difference in the world. On the other, he racked up a lot of criminal charges and was tried twice in the murder of a young woman. He was certainly handsome, but his legacy of equal treatment for all seems compromised by his actions. Fall in love with his ideals, definitely, but beware of falling in love with the man.

QUOTABLES

"Huey could take street-gang types and give them a social consciousness."
Oakland County Supervisor John George

"To us, Huey Newton was a hero. The Black Panthers were a thing to identify with along with Malcolm X and Martin Luther King."
Fred DePalm, witness at the scene of Newton's death

"Huey P. Newton is the baddest motherf*cker ever to set foot inside of history. Huey has a very special meaning to black people, because for four hundred years black people have been wanting to do exactly what Huey Newton did, that is, to stand up in front of the most deadly tentacle of the white racist power structure, and to defy that deadly tentacle, and to tell that tentacle that he will not accept the aggression and the brutality, and that if he is moved against, he will retaliate in kind."
Fred DePalm, witness at the scene of Newton's death

"You can kill my body, but you can't kill my soul. My soul will live forever!"
Newton's reported dying words

BENAZIR BHUTTO

"the daughter of Pakistan"

VITAL STATS

YEARS: *1953 – 2007*

COUNTRY OF ORIGIN: *Pakistan*

AREA OF INFLUENCE: *Politics*

STYLE OF SEDUCTION:
Fightin' for your rights

No 50

The first female leader of a modern Muslim country, Benazir Bhutto was active in Pakistani politics until she was assassinated in 2007. Noted for her peacemaking efforts in a country torn between ancient Islamic values and democratic ideals, she strove to modernize the traditionalist state.

→ BHUTTO'S LIFE STORY

Benazir Bhutto was born into the comforts and challenges of Pakistani aristocracy—a solid platform on which to build a political career. The daughter of Zulfikar Ali Bhutto, who ran Pakistan for six years in the 1970s, she was bred to be her father's successor in a family whose entire livelihood revolved around politics. Heading first to Harvard in the United States (at the young age of sixteen!), then to Oxford in the UK, she racked up two liberal arts degrees, which included studies in philosophy and economics.

Upon her homecoming from Oxford, however, her father was arrested and she, too, was made a functional prisoner under house arrest. The military coup that overthrew her father's governance went so far as to hang him in 1979, and Bhutto spent her next five years in captivity, isolated either in her home or in jail. She was eventually "allowed" exile in 1984. Just a few years later, the martial law under which she had been punished was lifted, and she returned to her native country.

Bhutto jumped into the trenches to voice her concerns about Pakistan's President Zia and began reshaping her father's Pakistan People's Party (PPP). Elected cochairwoman of the party with her mother, she was then elected prime minister of Pakistan in 1988, in the country's first free election following Zia's death.

Bhutto led the new coalition government for two years but was being kicked out of office on charges of corruption. She eventually reclaimed Pakistani leadership in 1993. By 1996, though, her coalition government was dismissed by the new president, Farooq Leghari, who had deemed the PPP illegitimate. She left the country and remained ostracized for years, as Pervez Musharraf took charge in a coup d'état. Finally, in 2007, Musharraf granted her amnesty for the corruption charges that had kept her down for so long, and discussion commenced about a power-sharing deal between her and the president. Just when things started looking up, however, Bhutto was killed in a suicide attack, the final of several attempts on her life. She was fifty-four.

Of her husband, senator and businessman Asif Ali Zardari, Bhutto told a Pakistani Parliament senator, "Time will prove he is the Nelson Mandela of Pakistan." Though her husband was controversial, his own power and influence came close to rivaling hers—a quality that made them great partners. Even more impressively, this power couple (who ended up spending most of their time behind bars or in exile together) fought fiercely on behalf of each other. Rarely did it appear that one was jealous of the other's power, and how often does that happen? Maybe even more amazing is that the duo had an arranged marriage; they met for the first time just days before their engagement began.

A CORRUPT LEADER?

In the course of her political career, Benazir Bhutto was accused again and again of corruption, including allegations that she stole $1.5 million from the Pakistani government. Bhutto consistently disputed these claims, but mistrust of her leadership style continues to cast a shadow over her legacy. Whatever the truth may be, Bhutto will never be accused of not making an impact in the world.

CATHOLIC SCHOOLGIRL

It's hard to picture the dignified Benazir Bhutto in navy knee socks and a plaid miniskirt, but the prime minister was indeed a Catholic schoolgirl at one time. Until she was sent off to college at sixteen, she attended various Catholic schools throughout Pakistan, learning to bake cakes of *Cake Boss* quality and also, presumably, learning how to avoid the harsh admonitions of the nuns. It didn't take long, fortunately, for all that primness to wear off.

No naughty business.

→ WHY SHE MATTERS

With some help from her father's political experience, Benazir Bhutto succeeded in fighting her way through the ranks of the male-dominated Islamic political system to take her place as the first female prime minister of Pakistan. That *she did it* (no matter how many times she got thrown out) shines as a beacon of hope for Muslim women throughout the Middle East. Her confidence and take-charge attitude have also set an example to women of all countries and ethnicities: Simple belief in your own strengths can get the job done.

❖ BEST FEATURE: **Her grace under pressure.**
Bhutto didn't agree with the extremist laws that her people had been subjected to for so long, and she was accustomed to the chaos that often resulted from taking a stand. Yet she let nothing, not even attempted murder after attempted murder, stand in the way of her ambition. No matter what battle she was fighting, she always did it with poise and charm.

❖ HEAT FACTOR: **Benazir Bhutto rocked the world with her unique combination of brains, beauty, and confidence.**

1 2 3 4 5

Citing Margaret Thatcher as her role model, Benazir Bhutto was nothing if not authoritative—perhaps to the point of arrogance, depending on whom you ask. But her tendency to be demanding was nothing in comparison to the magnetic ambition the woman radiated when she walked into a room. Bhutto was frequently photographed with a white headscarf covering most of her reddish brown locks. Even with her looks somewhat obscured, however, she always made an impression.

QUOTABLES

"Bhutto represents everything the fundamentalists hate—a powerful, highly educated woman operating in a man's world, seemingly unafraid to voice her independent views and, indeed, seemingly unafraid of anything, including the very real possibility that one day someone might succeed in killing her because of who she is."
British journalist Ginny Dougary

"She believes she is the chosen one, that she is the daughter of Bhutto and everything else is secondary."
Pakistani corporate lawyer Feisal Naqvi

"Benazir Bhutto was a woman of immense personal courage and bravery. . . . She risked everything in her attempt to win democracy in Pakistan, and she has been assassinated by cowards afraid of democracy."
UK Prime Minister Gordon Brown

FURTHER READING

The 50 Greatest Love Letters of All Time, edited by David H. Lowenherz (Crown, 2002)

Behind the Palace Doors: Five Centuries of Sex, Adventure, Vice, Treachery, and Folly from Royal Britain, by Michael Farquhar (Random House, 2011)

Doomed Queens: Royal Women Who Met Bad Ends, from Cleopatra to Princess Di, by Kris Waldherr (Three Rivers Press, 2008)

The Greatest Stories Never Told: 100 Tales from History to Astonish, Bewilder, and Stupify, by Rick Beyer (HarperResource, 2003)

A History of the World in 100 Objects, by Neil MacGregor (Viking Press, 2011)

The Intimate Sex Lives of Famous People, by Irving Wallace, Amy Wallace, David Wallechinsky, and Sylvia Wallace (Feral House, 2008)

Lives of the Artists: Masterpieces, Messes (and What the Neighbors Thought), by Kathleen Krull

Lives of the Scientists: Experiments, Explosions (and What the Neighbors Thought), by Kathleen Krull and Kathryn Hewitt (Sandpiper, 2011)

Napoleon's Privates: 2,500 Years of History Unzipped, by Tony Perrottet (It Books, 2008)

Notorious Royal Marriages: A Juicy Journey Through Nine Centuries of Dynasty, Destiny, and Desire, by Leslie Carroll (NAL Trade, 2010)

Queen, Empress. Concubine: Fifty Women Rulers from the Queen of Sheba to Catherine the Great, by Claudia Gold (Quercus, 2009)

Royal Pains: A Rogues' Gallery of Brats, Brutes, and Bad Seeds, by Leslie Carroll (NAL Trade, 2011)

Royal Romances: Titillating Tales of Passion and Power in the Palaces of Europe, by Leslie Carroll (NAL Trade, 2012)

Secret Lives of the First Ladies: What Your Teachers Never Told You About the Women of the White House, by Cormac O'Brien (Quirk Books, 2009)

Secret Lives of Great Artists: What Your Teachers Never Told You About Famous Master Painters and Illustrators, by Elizabeth Lunday (Quirk Books, 2008)

Secret Lives of Great Authors: What Your Teachers Never Told You About Famous Novelists, Poets, and Playwrights, by Robert Schnakenberg (Quirk Books, 2008)

Secret Lives of the U.S. Presidents: What Your Teachers Never Told You About the Men of the White House, by Cormac O'Brien (Quirk Books, 2003)

Sex with Kings: 500 Years of Adultery, Power, Rivalry, and Revenge, by Eleanor Herman (William Morrow, 2005)

Sex with the Queen: 900 Years of Vile Kings, Virile Lovers, and Passionate Politics, by Eleanor Herman (William Morrow, 2007)

A Treasury of Great American Scandals: Tantalizing True Tales of Historic Misbehavior by the Founding Fathers and Others Who Let Freedom Swing, by Michael Farquhar (Penguin Books, 2003)

A Treasury of Royal Scandals: The Shocking True Stories of History's Wickedest, Weirdest, Most Wanton Kings, Queens, Tsars, Popes, and Emperors, by Michael Farquhar (Penguin Books, 2001)

Writers Gone Wild: The Feuds, Frolics, and Follies of Literature's Great Adventurers, Drunkards, Lovers, Iconoclasts, and Misanthropes, by Bill Peschel (Perigee Trade, 2010)

INDEX